THE
COFFEE
RUN

THE
COFFEE
RUN

And Other Internship Need-to-Knows

SYDNEY N. FULKERSON

INKSHARES

Published by Inkshares Inc., San Francisco, California
www.inkshares.com

Edited and designed by Girl Friday Productions
www.girlfridayproductions.com

Cover design by Danielle Fiorella
Illustrations by Benjamin Wade

ISBN: 9781941758434
Library of Congress Control Number: 2015939061

First edition

Printed in the United States of America

CONTENTS

THE INTRO

This book is not about coffee. Coffee is only the beginning. As a three-time, borderline "pro" intern, I've experienced just about everything—from the most mundane tasks to the most thought-provoking responsibilities. I've received a lot of questions from friends and students about my internship experiences. To help convey what I've learned, I did some research on internships to back up my advice. I came across formal textbooks, poorly written blogs, and opinionated forums that were far from the truth. After unsuccessfully locating an honest yet informative internship book for students, I was inspired.

I landed my first internship at age eighteen for a women's designer in New York City. I would have considered myself the "do anything and everything" type of intern, knowing that everyone has to start somewhere. I learned to look at a coffee run in ninety-degree humidity as an opportunity rather than a punishment. My second internship was for a high-end, women's and men's designer, also in New York City, but to my disappointment that resulted in my using less brainpower than last summer's Friday afternoon Japanese takeout errand. I craved challenges and responsibilities that were, unfortunately, overlooked by caffeine-addicted clients and disorganized employees. Some days it took everything in me to not break down, until I adjusted my mindset and realized that figuring out what you *don't* want to do is just as important as figuring out what you *do* want to do. Luckily my third go-round, as a marketing intern for a Los Angeles activewear designer, turned into the best internship I could have asked for. From managing all of the company's social media accounts to developing the designer's social responsibility program, I was treated like an employee from day one. An internship isn't quite the real world—you aren't expected to already know everything because you're there to learn, and everybody knows you will make mistakes. You get to figure out what you like, what you don't like, what you're awesome at, and what you more or less suck at. Internships help you test the waters before committing to a career. As today's job world grows more competitive and internships become part of a mandatory education curriculum, it's important to learn how to master your internship from the get-go. I've been right where you are—countless times. I know what it's like: the excitement, the stress, the uncertainty. You aren't alone!

The Coffee Run: And Other Internship Need-to-Knows is the what-to-do and how-to-do-it guide that will prepare you from pre- to postinternship in any industry. This book is for everyone! It's for guys and gals, accountants and engineers, dentists and doctors, and any other industry. It follows you to your first week, helps you break out of common intern stereotypes, and shows you how to be a standout. This book is the resource I wish I'd had before my internships—the book you will actually *want* to read. Don't let the coffee get cold—dive in today to begin making the most of your internship and beyond.

THE SEARCH

Only those who will risk going too far can
possibly find out how far they can go.

—T. S. Eliot

It's the start of spring semester. Trevor, a college sophomore, is already thinking about summer break and how he should spend it. Thoughts of sleeping in till noon and video game marathons are quickly interrupted by the realization that he needs an internship. Exiting his opened Facebook tab, Trevor decides he wants to research family practice internships for experience in his psychology major. After several minutes of staring at his search engine, he shakes his head: "Where do I begin?"

I'll tell you exactly where to begin: with yourself, and by asking questions. What do you want out of an internship? What are your skills? What do you want to improve on? Are you willing and able to do an unpaid internship? Do you want to work out of state? Out of the country? Your honest answers to these questions will become your framework for your internship search and help you hone in on the perfect position. Once you've taken all of these questions into consideration, begin creating one of my favorite things: a list.

When I began my search for an internship, I knew I wanted an out-of-state, paid internship, and I wanted to work for a smaller, up-and-coming company. I wanted to have a direct impact. Most important, I wanted to like the company's product and believe in its mission.

Sound specific? Well, it was. My answers to the questions on my list led me to the best internship I could have ever sought out. With research, patience, and persistence, you, too, can locate (and land) an internship tailored to fulfill your interests and needs.

Because my internships were so fulfilling, my friends started to ask me, "How do I find an internship?" Eventually, other students—even strangers—started to ask me, too. Once you know what you want out of an internship, how do you find it? My response is simple: *start early, ask questions, make a list, email prospects, and follow up.*

START EARLY

Begin your search ten months before you want to start an internship. You might think ten months is a crazy amount of time when you can't even wrap your head around what you're doing next weekend, but I can assure you that you'll need more time than you think to research internships. Starting ten months out will give you plenty of time to brainstorm, polish your résumé, create cover letters specific to the company you are interested in, and stay ahead of the game when it comes to securing the internship.

If you're too early, don't despair. Several times, I emailed a prospective employer almost too far in advance and received feedback stating that the company was not looking to hire interns until the first of the year. If this happens to you, let the employer know that you will look forward to touching base when applications are being accepted. This shows the potential employer that you are actively seeking out positions. If you are the kind of intern they are looking for, they might possibly adjust their application date.

ASK QUESTIONS

Your best resources for finding an internship might be right around you—you never know until you ask. The minute you put yourself out there is when you will discover opportunities all around you. Begin your internship hunt by asking the people you know for connections. People are your number-one resource. Your living, breathing networking system will give you answers that you cannot always find on the Internet or at career fairs.

High school teachers and college professors: You might ask, "Look, I know it didn't *look* like I was paying attention in your class, but I swear I was. So, any advice about how to score an awesome internship?" Well, maybe you should skip that first sentence, but your teachers and professors, particularly if they teach the subject you're interested in, will be a wealth of information.

Immediate and extended family members: Make a list of your family's jobs. Do any of them match up with what you want to do? Ask them, "Can you sit down with me to discuss how I can get my foot in the door? I'd really like to start working on my internship search."

Friends and friends of friends: Make a list of your friends' jobs and their parents' jobs. Or just ask around: "Doesn't your mom work for that one guy at that one place? Yeah, can you ask her if I can have his email?"

Current boss and coworkers, if you're employed: Your current job—yeah, that one at the mall—might not be your dream job, but your boss and coworkers may be able to make connections for you. Tell everyone, "I am interested in looking for an internship next summer. Do you know anyone who works in the XYZ industry that I could speak to for guidance?"

Professionals in the industry: For example, if you are interested in an editorial internship for a magazine, begin with contacting an editor of a local magazine: "I'm incredibly interested in this industry, but I'd like to get a feel for it before I commit. Do you happen to know any available internships in this field?"

Most of the time, the people you connect with will be more than happy to assist you by giving you advice and potential contacts. Ask them some preliminary questions:

1. What do you look for in an intern?
2. What qualifications are required for this internship?
3. Do you have any recommendations for potential interns?

Their answers to these questions will be a good foundation for your internship search and will show you what skills or qualifications you should highlight when you apply. Don't waste time searching and applying for internships that do not match your skill set. That's why it's important to build this foundation before contacting potential employers.

THEMUSE.COM

Although networking is my number-one recommendation for locating and landing an internship, the Muse is a website that I highly recommend. The site features job posts, which you can filter to show only internship search results. The Muse also offers career and interview advice, free classes for essential skills, the chance to browse offices before you apply, and much more. This is a site whose e-newsletter I actually read because the advice is so rock solid—for students, interns, and graduates.

MAKE A LIST

Before you contact employers directly, go back to the drawing board for some serious brainstorming and list making. This step is commonly overlooked, especially among students who wait till the last minute to start searching.

+ LIST COMPANIES THAT FIT YOUR INTERESTS

Really think about it. What company do you admire? Where can you see yourself dedicating several months of your time? What aspect of an industry do you enjoy most (or think you will enjoy most)? When it comes to searching for internships, you will be so much happier if you take the time to create a written list of companies that *actually* interest you. Even if the company does not have a current internship listed, and even if you don't know if it has an established internship program, write its name down anyway.

Believe it or not, my most rewarding internship experience was for a company that at the time didn't have an established internship program. The company responded by asking, "What kind of internship are you looking for?" Take advantage of that response if you get one! It means opportunity, flexibility, and negotiating—you get to decide for yourself the kind of atmosphere into which you want to submerse yourself.

+ LIST COMPANY CONTACT INFORMATION

Having the Internet at our fingertips makes it easy to search for company contact information. Write down each company's contact email. If the company is small, aim high and see if you can find the email address of the CEO, founder, or vice president. You have a better chance of getting in touch with someone if you bypass the human resources (HR) folks and put your résumé directly into the hands of the person you really want to be reading it. If the company is large, you will likely have to start with HR or the head of the department you're interested in. For some companies, the bigwigs will be out of reach. Be strategic about the people to whom you send your résumé, and spend time learning the company's structure. Make sure you locate a specific contact to whom you can address your email and cover letter.

If you cannot determine a name and email address online, pick up the phone. Call the person at the front desk, who is probably able to provide a wealth of information. Ask for the name and email of the person in charge of the department you want to contact. If you are given a name but not an email address, ask to whom you should send your email.

Do your best to try to locate a specific person's email and avoid the company's general email (e.g., info@company.com). As a last resort, use the company's general email but address it specifically. Put "ATTN: Name of person" in the subject line so that the email will be forwarded.

NAVIGATING CORPORATE STRUCTURE

If you're pursuing a national corporation, be careful! Be sure to write down the correct email address for the specific location where you are wanting to intern. If you are interested in applying for an internship in your local city, do not write down the email of the corporate office in Atlanta. Once the corporate office reads about an inquiry for a position in another city, your email will be trashed. Send your email to a corporate headquarters only if you want to intern at that location and you have the name of someone to contact.

As you make your list, take notes on why the company interests you as well as the qualifications required and anything specific about the internship. The more notes you take on a company of interest, the more honest and knowledgeable your email is going to be. (See "The Cover Letter" for more information.) Spend the time preparing to ensure that once you do contact prospects, you are already a standout candidate.

EMAIL YOUR PROSPECTS

Now you're ready to reach out to companies about interning for them. Several parts are involved in doing that. Let's break down what you need to include in this "Hire me as an intern, please" email.

SPELL-CHECK IT

Before you send your email, make a best friend with spell-check. You can spend hours on your research, résumé, and cover letter, but whenever you send an email full of spelling and grammatical errors, you can bet that it will be immediately trashed. For example, no one wants to suffer through your misuse of *their* versus *they're*. Spelling and grammatical errors hint at laziness and are oftentimes associated with unintelligence. Don't let yourself be labeled like that.

+ THE RÉSUMÉ

Beginning in high school, you should create a document that lists your education, experiences, skills, and honors. A résumé, in short, sums up your strengths and makes you look qualified. It is the document that potential employers look at to assess your qualifications.

I once heard a speaker in a finance class say, "When I look at résumés, my motive is to put as many in the trash—or in today's world, delete as many from my email—as possible. That way I am left with only the best of the best to review. There has to be something on that résumé within the first three seconds of my reviewing that is different enough to separate it from the rest." His advice is blunt yet incredibly helpful. The larger the corporation, the more résumés it sorts through. Because of this, large companies often have a similar motive: to save time by dismissing as many résumés as possible.

Internships are becoming more and more competitive, which shouldn't intimidate you but, instead, motivate you to be more of a standout candidate. How will your résumé set you apart within the first two or three seconds? Focus first on the strengths that you believe differentiate you from other students. Such strengths could include the following:

- Maintaining an excellent grade point average (GPA 3.8 or above)
- Working a part-time job while being a full-time student
- Holding an officer or leader position
- Graduating early
- Participating in extracurricular activities (e.g., captain of the tennis team, president of the French club)
- Winning scholarships and honors
- Studying, speaking, reading, or writing a second language

Unfortunately, listing a *winning personality* under extra-curricular activities will not advance your résumé—keep that for your interview. At this stage, you want to create a unique résumé that makes a potential employer say "Wow, what a candidate" or something along those lines.

Follow these tips to make your résumé a standout:

- Keep the confidence but lose the ego. Some students feel uncomfortable writing about their honors, skills, and experiences because they worry they'll sound boastful. Well, don't. Your résumé should be objective and honest, and list your most recent experiences and strongest skills first.
- Make sure there are absolutely zero spelling errors. Seriously—not one. Have several people proof your résumé for you. Sometimes it takes numerous sets of eyes to catch the small mistakes.
- List any experience, job, or award from your *past* in *past* tense.
- Make your résumé visually appealing and easily legible (e.g., use subheadings, bold font).
- Attempt to keep your résumé to one page. (For extensive experience, such as several relevant jobs and internships, you may need more than one page.)
- Don't be too wordy—keep your language simple yet effective. Stick to résumé power words (e.g., *exceeded*, *innovated*, *mentored*) to prevent language from being repetitive or boring. An example of some of these power words can be found at www.careerrealism.com/top-resume-words.

PROFESSIONAL RÉSUMÉ SERVICES

I have revised my résumé more times than I can count. The more people I ask to look it over, the more edits I make. Eventually I realized that this revising could literally go on forever, so I decided to go straight to someone who professionally revises and edits these documents: a résumé service. Yes, they do exist. Search on the Web for "résumé services"—the number of people whose sole job it is to make your résumé the best it can possibly be will shock you. Given the financial investment for using these services—hundreds of dollars—you may need to hold back on the caramel lattes and personalized Nike Frees, but it will serve you best in the long run. I used a résumé service that I found through a mutual friend, and I was blown away by how awesome my résumé looked. My skills and experiences obviously didn't change, but the adjusted verbiage and professional layout were a night-and-day difference from my old résumé that I would not have had if I had not invested in this service.

Example of one-page résumé format.

Full Name

Current mailing address | School email | Cell phone number
Seeking Position as Marketing Intern | PR Intern | Sales Intern

EDUCATION

INTERN UNIVERSITY, City, State | Major | Expected Graduation Date
Honor Society | Overall GPA: x.x

STUDENT HIGHLIGHTS

- This is your section to showcase how awesome you are.
- List five to seven facts and highlights about yourself that make you feel the most proud.
- Keep it concise and to the point.
- For example: "Granted Political Science Scholarship for Intern University, 2013"
- Or even "Early graduation; consecutive Dean's List, 2011-2014

SKILLS

TECHNOLOGY SKILLS
- Microsoft: Office & Windows
- Adobe: InDesign, Photoshop, Acrobat

LEADERSHIP
- Editor of school magazine
- Organize & manage team meetings once a month
- President of campus Study Abroad

WORK EXPERIENCE

CAMPUS BOOKSTORE, City, State | August 2013-2015
- Sold 25% more textbooks than minimum sales goal
- Managed bookstore's social media accounts
- Grew social media followers by 20 percent

THAT SALES COMPANY, City, State | Summer 2013
- Increased sales by 50 percent with major client accounts
- Managed company reorders
- Exceeded seasonal sales goals

+ THE COVER LETTER

When you apply for an internship, in most cases the body of the email will serve as your cover letter. A cover letter states your reasons for reaching out. Keep it short and to the point, but evoke enough interest that the reader will want to finish reading it and click to see your résumé.

The most important thing about writing a cover letter is this: *Personalize*. When I say *personalize*, I mean that your cover letter should include information relevant to the employer to whom you are emailing. The worst preintern move is to copy and paste a generic cover letter that you use for every company. For starters, that's lazy. Second, a cover letter should explain why you believe that you're capable and deserving of this particular internship. Include reasons X, Y, and Z, or else have your email join the hundreds of others in the trash.

Use your previous research to your advantage. Employ the language you found on any prospective employer's website, especially from the "About" page, to show that you can relate with the organization. Everybody who reads your submission will pick up on this—they want interns to have prior knowledge about their mission and values. One way to demonstrate your understanding is by picking up on buzzwords. For example, Zappos is known for the company's enthusiastic culture. The company created a "WOW Philosophy" that is summed up with the belief that "At Zappos, anything worth doing is worth doing with WOW." If you apply for an internship at Zappos, it would be smart to include how you have that "WOW" quality and how you would adapt to the company's highly acclaimed culture.

As far as cover letter structure goes, here are six steps to follow:

- Address the letter to a specific contact, then begin with a brief introduction (e.g., "Dear Mark: My name is Chris Wolf, and I am currently studying journalism at Intern University, New York."). Include your name; current education (list the school location if not noted in the name of the school); major and minor, if applicable.
- State that you're inquiring about an internship position for a specific date (e.g., summer 2015).
- State why you deserve the internship, then use your buzzwords: "As you can see from my résumé (attached), I exhibit X, Y, and Z, which aligns with your company's mission of..."
- Include your contact information (email, phone number).
- List the documents you have enclosed, including your résumé and any recommendations.
- Choose an appropriate closing: "Sincerely, (your name)" is an old standard that is appropriate for any employer. "Best, (your name)" is a more modern sign-off that is also accepted by most employers. "Regards, (your name)" is another option but can sometimes come off as too formal; if you are applying for a fun, upbeat company, closing your letter with "Regards" may not be the best option.

There is no perfect, absolutely correct, or definitely incorrect way to construct a cover letter. At a minimum, include the preceding bullet points. Word everything in the way you feel represents you best. After all, you're selling yourself.

The following is an example of a cover letter layout I have used in the past (company name has been changed):

Dear Mark:

My name is Sydney Fulkerson. I am currently studying merchandising, apparel, and textiles with a minor in business administration at the University of Kentucky. I am reaching out in regard to Lloyd & Inc.'s Summer 2015 Sales Internship opportunity. I am interested in your company because of X, Y, and Z.

As you can see from my résumé, I have more than four years of experience in sales and marketing. I believe my organizational and communication skills would be of value to Lloyd & Inc. in developing and maintaining client relationships. My experience in graphic design and visual merchandising would also benefit Lloyd & Inc.'s mission to link the brand to the consumer interactively.

Please accept the attached résumé and recommendation. I am available at your earliest convenience to discuss the sales intern position scheduled to begin in May 20XX. I can be reached at s_fulkerson@xxxxxxxx.com or 555.555.5555.

Thank you in advance for your time and consideration.

Sincerely,

Sydney N. Fulkerson

Enc.

+ THE EMAIL

You've proofread your résumé and cover letter. Now you're ready to construct the actual email and hit "Send." Here are a few tips.

++ YOUR EMAIL ADDRESS

Send the email from your school email address if possible. If not, make sure your personal email is appropriate (your seventh-grade AIM email is probably not okay). Double-check that the email account matches the one listed on your résumé and cover letter. Consistency is important.

++ THE SUBJECT LINE

The subject line of the email should be brief and relevant. If the internship you seek is for a specific position, include that in the subject line (e.g., "Marketing Internship Inquiry"). If you aren't applying for a specific spot, leave the subject line a bit more generalized, such as "Internship Inquiry for Summer 2015."

++ THE BODY OF THE EMAIL

Make sure the font and font size are legible, not obnoxious. Use Comic Sans and you might as well throw in some classic clip art and 3-D shadow boxes. Baskerville Old Face, Palatino, or Times New Roman are easy to read and professional in appearance.

Constructing emails to send to potential employers is exciting. You may receive a response or you may never receive one, even after a follow-up email. Whatever the outcome, if you know that you represented yourself in the best way that you could, then you have already achieved quite a bit. Put yourself out there—it's the best thing you can do for internship searches.

IS YOUR SOCIAL MEDIA APPROPRIATE?

Before you hit "Send," clean up your social media accounts. When employers receive your email, the first thing they do is search for you on Facebook! They want to see what you look like, what your interests are, and how you present yourself. During my second internship, one of the salespeople called me over to her desk and said, "Hey, Sydney, this gal just emailed us her résumé. She's from Louisville and worked at the same shop you did. Do you know her?" She showed me three different Facebook accounts of females with the same name. I pointed to the right one. After she closed out the other tabs, she began to do some serious stalking.

As social media use continues to grow, our privacy levels are at an all-time low. Make sure to delete any inappropriate pictures, statuses, tweets, and so on that an employer could see. If you'd rather not be stalked, play around with privacy settings. If you are unsure if something is or isn't appropriate, think of it this way: Would you be okay with an entire company seeing it? (You may now go back and remove that spring break cover photo.) Be smart.

THE FOLLOW-UP EMAIL

Sending a follow-up email is (debatably) what could make or break your chances of getting that internship you badly want. Emails can land mysteriously in spam folders, be deleted accidentally, or be read and forgotten about in minutes. While students tend to avoid following up because it feels pushy—or because they assume they didn't land the position—I cannot reiterate enough the importance of a follow-up. Unless an internship application or a company's website specifically notes something like "If you have not heard back, it is because you did not get the internship," then by all means follow up. Some companies receive hundreds of applications and internship inquiries each *day*. So an HR department staffer who notices your follow-up email after reading your well-constructed cover letter may take the time to address your inquiry.

Now that you've emailed several employers, keep track of who you sent an email to as well as the date you sent it. Wait about ten days before sending a follow-up email.

Your follow-up email can be short, like this one:

SUBJECT: Follow-up Inquiry for Summer 2015 Internship

Dear Bryan:

I'm reaching out to confirm that you received the cover letter I sent ten days ago. I'm still incredibly interested in an internship for the summer of 2015 and look forward to hearing from you.
Sincerely,
Sydney N. Fulkerson
(555)-555-5555

You could receive a "Sorry, not interested" response (I have, multiple times), or you could receive an email saying, "Apologies for the delayed response. Your résumé looks like you could be a good candidate. Let's set up a time next week for an interview." If you still don't receive a response, try a phone call—you have a chance if you can reach someone that way. Don't give up, stay positive, and keep trying.

. . .

The search for an internship is an exciting process filled with possibilities. The outcome of your search is highly dependent on the amount of time, energy, and research you put into it. It's never too soon to begin brainstorming what you want out of an internship, what interests and skills you want to exhibit during an internship, and what makes you a standout candidate.

Always remember that passion drives persistence. The more nos you receive from potential employers, the more yeses you are likely to elicit. If I gave up my search after every no that I received, you would not be reading this book. Once you locate and develop your passion, your persistence will guide you to opportunities you might not have yet imagined.

THE SEARCH TAKEAWAYS

Ask Questions
- Use people as your number-one resource in your search for potential internships.

Make a List
- List companies that fit your interests, and list their contact information.

The Résumé
- Focus your résumé on what makes you stand out from every other candidate.

The Cover Letter
- Personalize! Use company buzzwords.

The Email
- Proofread—a lot.

The Follow-up Email
- Sometimes people need a friendly reminder of how awesome a candidate you are. Make sure they know that.

THE INTERVIEW

One important key to success is self-confidence. An
important key to self-confidence is preparation."
—Arthur Ashe

S ydney, can you see us?"
 I straightened up in my chair and made eye contact
 with the man and woman on the screen.
 "I can. Are you able to see me?"
 They took a few seconds to respond, and I heard their voices
before their lips moved.

OH NO! THE AUDIO IS OFF

Nothing is more distracting during a video interview than hearing one thing and watching the interviewers' mouths move seconds too late. Worse, the interviewers were sitting at the longest
conference table I had ever seen, with their heads tilted up and
eyes fixed on a screen above them. I suddenly realized that they
were staring at me on a large flat-screen TV. Awkward. My first
virtual interview.
 A few crucial things are important to keep in mind during
an interview. Whether it's via Skype or another VoIP program, in
person, or over the phone, it's better to be overprepared than not

prepared at all. Here's an overview, based on my experience, of interview need-to-knows:

+ ANTICIPATE QUESTIONS BEFORE THE INTERVIEW

Before the call began, I had spent a solid hour and a half preparing for this interview. To my surprise, I found that my college's career center had interview rooms where students could practice mock interviews. After I reserved one, I got to work.

First, I printed off a copy of my résumé for easy reference.

Be sure you know your résumé like the back of your hand. Study it ruthlessly to the point that you could rewrite it without referring to the old one. Most questions interviewers ask come directly from your résumé—they want to get to know you better than bullet-point phrases on a piece of paper. The good thing about this is that you can anticipate their questions and think about the answers before your actual interview.

At times, however, the interviewer will throw you for a loop and ask you a thoughtful question that a bullet point on your résumé just can't answer. Expect to be asked open-ended questions. Your interviewer is likely to ask these questions:

Why should we choose you over every other applicant for this business internship?

What is your biggest strength, your biggest weakness?

What do you hope to get out of this internship?

How did you manage your time as a full-time student with a part-time job?

Tell me about a time when you made a mistake and how you handled it.

The list of potential questions is infinite—so while you can't know every single question you will be asked in an interview, you can still prepare answers to the ones you *do* anticipate. One of the best interview questions I have ever heard is this: If someone were to walk into this room right now and say that there is an emergency that you must attend to, what would you tell me as you're being yanked out the door and I'm asking you why you deserve this position? Really makes you think, doesn't it? Brainstorming answers to a handful of questions before your internship interviews will not only better prepare you, but it also will ease your nerves.

If you're not sure what an interviewer might ask, ask your friends what questions they have been asked in interviews. Call a company's HR department, introduce yourself, and ask if they have a minute to tell you their top-three favorite interview questions—after all, they do the hiring.

+ DO YOUR RESEARCH

As I prepped, I also researched the company as much as I could. I took note of its mission, clients, growth—everything I could locate online.

Hopefully, you already did this when you were developing your cover letter. It's still a good idea to brush up on what you know. Focus on the organization's mission and vision, who "they" are, what they do, their clients, their competitors. Research it, then write it down. Make sure you can refer to this information during the interview. Take notes in an easy-to-read, bulletproof format to help you quickly locate and remember specific information.

Keep up with your industry in the media. Stay informed by reading periodicals, magazines, online forums—anything that could better prepare you. Take note of industry trends, verbiage, buzzwords, competitors, and anything else that you believe could benefit you. Start following important leaders, companies, and influencers in your industry on Twitter, Facebook, and Instagram to stay up-to-date and ahead of the game. It makes you look *really* good when you spit out a current fact about the industry and catch your interviewer off guard. Go that extra step.

+ AVOID WORD VOMIT

Now let's get back to my awkward interview. After we said hello, the guy talked briefly about the company. I made sure to maintain a good posture and a smile, and I tried really hard not to let the delayed audio distract me. The interviewers' first question was one I had anticipated: "Tell me about yourself." *Classic question.* When you answer an interview question like this, *avoid word vomit.*

Vomit. Eww, I hate the word, too—sort of like how interviewers hate when candidates spit out ridiculous run-on sentences.

Keep your answers concise, effective, and to the point. Most people really have to practice this. When they get nervous, they tend to ramble. As a matter of fact, some people just do not know when to shut up—for example, when you are asked about the most rewarding class you had in college and you end up rambling about your first childhood bike accident and that trip you took to the Grand Canyon last summer. You laugh, but this happens in interviews all the time. Stay on track and get to the point.

First practice answering interview questions with your friends and family. Once you are comfortable with that, move on to answering questions with classmates or professors who you don't know very well. You'll be surprised how different your answers can sound in front of different people.

+ ASK QUESTIONS, TOO

About twenty-five long minutes later, the interviewers finally turned the table on me. "It's been great getting to know you, Sydney. Do you have any questions for us?"

Yes. Why does your audio suck? Of course, I didn't dare ask that.

Most interviewers ask at the end of an interview if you have any questions for them. Always say yes and proceed with a question—it's your last chance to leave a memorable impression. Make sure it's a good, open-ended question because yes and no answers create awkward silences. To ensure that your questions are engaging, refer to the following list:

- What does a typical day for an intern look like?
- How would you describe the company's work environment?
- What is the quality that your company has that is different from your competitors?
- What growth do you see for this company in the next five years?
- What are the first three words that best describe this company, and why?

If an interviewer does not ask if you have any questions, try to ask one. Say, "Excuse me. If you have time, I have a question I would like to ask before we end the interview." Chances are the interviewer does have time and is interested in what you have to ask. At this point, you have extended the interview, so you better have a great question prepared!

+ REMEMBER INTERVIEW ETIQUETTE

I am not here to teach you manners, but I will briefly reiterate the importance of basic interview etiquette. I am continuously shocked by the gum-chewing, word-slurring, eyes-wandering student who sways into an interview as if the internship had already been landed. Spit out the gum, articulate your words, and use consistent eye contact. Basic etiquette is common sense—or so I thought. To ensure that your interview etiquette is up to par, abide by the following pointers:

- Don't have coffee breath: Eat a mint, or ten, before you go into an interview; it's common courtesy.
- Mirror the interviewer: People feel most comfortable talking to people who speak and sound like them. If your interviewer talks fast, speed up your answers. If she enjoys telling stories, tell one.
- Maintain eye contact: People have a habit of staring off into space when thinking of what to say. Consciously try to avoid that.
- Remember your posture: Sit up straight.
- Give a firm handshake: Guys, you are not trying to win an arm-wrestling contest. Gals, don't shake with a limp hand.
- Don't shake that leg: Don't do that nervous, quick, and—for some—habitual leg shake we all know. It's incredibly distracting and makes you look like you are in need of a bathroom.

We all have a tendency to alter our behavior when we know we are being watched, judged, and evaluated. An interview is no different. Be confident in yourself, and you will appear so during your interview. You can do this with practice, mental preparation, and really strong mints.

. . .

No interview is the same, and with every interview you will improve in one way or another. You do not have control over the setting of the interview, the questions you are asked, or the person interviewing you. You do, however, have control of the extent of your preparation, your positive mind-set, and how you present yourself. If you make a mistake, say something stupid, or say "um" after every word—take note, practice more, and move on to the next interview.

THE INTERVIEW TAKEAWAYS

Anticipate Questions Before the Interview
- Brainstorm questions before your interview to be better prepared and to ease your nerves.

Do Your Research
- Stay informed and knowledgeable about the industry in which you will be interviewing.

Avoid Word Vomit
- Keep your answers concise, effective, and to the point.

Ask Questions, Too
- Ask your interviewer questions in order to appear interested and to leave a memorable impression.

Remember Interview Etiquette
- Be confident, be courteous, and—for your sake and mine—remember good hygiene.

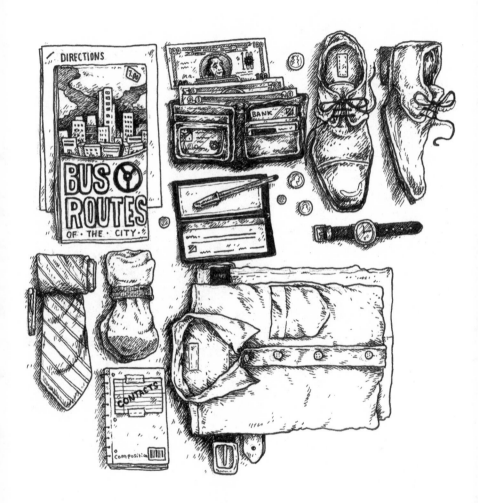

THE PREPARATION

Give me six hours to chop down a tree and I will spend the
first four sharpening the axe.
—Abraham Lincoln

During the summer of my last internship, I joined a gym
near the office. I happened to meet someone in a morning spinning class, and we quickly became friends. At
our coordinated workouts and Friday happy hours, we talked
about my current internship and her experiences as an intern. To
my surprise, I learned that she had a lot to say about internships
and how to prepare for one.

Marisa had found a second internship at a Boston mediation
center that completely sparked her interest. According to her
supervisor, her previous internship had turned her into "the fast-
est binder-maker east of the Mississippi," so Marisa was excited
that this second internship would be a step above setting the
copy machine to double-sided, collated, and stapled. The catch?
No pay.

It didn't take Marisa long to find out that nonprofits were
thrilled to hire students at no expense. But since she was craving
a challenging internship, she began to research, several months in
advance. She questioned how she could compensate for another
summer without pay. To her surprise, she learned that her university's career center provided extensive information on various

fellowships that funded unpaid internships—a financially struggling college student's dream come true.

It may feel like a stretch to think about finances months before your internship, but it's a necessary part of the preparations. If Marisa hadn't spent time researching at the career center, she would not have discovered the fellowship that funded her internship. As much as she wanted to break her binder-making record, Marisa had a different plan. Her drive to intern where she wanted along with her financial preparation led to the best internship ever.

. . .

Life would flash before our eyes (even faster than it already does) if we only focused on the future. There does come a time, however, when we have to spend time preparing for what lies ahead. From a budget, to housing accommodations, to your attire, there is a lot to consider before you start your internship. The better you prepare, the more confidence you'll have as an intern and the less you'll have to juggle while working forty-hour weeks. Nobody likes added stress before stepping into the world of interning. So let's begin with the fun stuff—finances!

BUDGET

Depending on your industry of interest, you could be faced with more unpaid internship options than paid ones. The fashion industry, for example, has hundreds of unpaid internships. Why? Because students are willing to work for free just to get their foot in the door—I was one of them—not to mention that employers are more than willing to accommodate that. When I moved to New York City at age nineteen, I thought that an unpaid internship was the least of my worries. That was until I realized that a lettuce leaf with half a cucumber cost about $12.

Whether you've landed an unpaid, paid, in-state, or out-of-state internship, tackle these budgeting tactics right away.

+ THE UNPAID INTERNSHIP

Working for months at a time without pay is tough. After my first internship, I made it a point to overestimate in the future how much I thought I would spend on food, transportation, and other wants and needs. Trust me: you don't want financial shortages to prevent you from making the most out of your internship. I don't believe that money buys happiness, but it sure makes affording $12 salads every day a bit easier.

Before you land an internship, try putting at least 20 percent of your earnings directly into a savings account. Start saving one year before you plan to start your next internship. It may not feel like substantial savings, but I promise it adds up.

Check out websites like CNN Money to compare prices of food, gas, housing, and so on between two cities. This will show you an estimate of how much more or less expensive the cost of living is from one city to another.

If you don't have a steady income and need ways to make up for lack of pay during an internship, consider the following:

- Work part-time during the week and on weekends.
- If you'll be interning for a larger company, look into scholarships the company might offer specifically for students.
- Seek out funding through your school and fellowships like Marisa did.
- Sell stuff you don't use anymore on eBay. (You laugh, but money is money!)

You can also inquire about a daily stipend. If your employer has already established that the internship is unpaid, ask for at least $20 a day to help accommodate for food and transportation. The worst they can say is no. Who knows, maybe your boss is in a great mood that afternoon and would be more than willing to support a money-hungry intern? Take the risk. You never know until you ask.

FREE LABOR

As internship programs and degrees requiring internships for credit increase, the options for internships are at an all-time high. But this also means more competition. Students needing internships and companies needing interns are all feeling the competitive edge. A common misconception about internships is that you work for free. Many times internship applications will offer "college credit" to compensate for not paying you.

According to the US Department of Labor, there is a test to determine if it is legal for you to intern for free.[1] The following six criteria must be met for the exclusion of intern pay:

The internship, even though it includes actual operation of the facilities of the employer, is similar to training that would be given in an educational environment; the internship experience is for the benefit of the intern; the intern does not displace regular employees but works under close supervision of existing staff; the employer that provides the training derives no immediate advantage from the activities of the intern, and on occasion its operations may actually be impeded; the intern is not necessarily entitled to a job at the conclusion of the internship; and the employer and the intern understand that the intern is not entitled to wages for the time spent in the internship.

The Department of Labor also states, "The more an internship program is structured around a classroom or academic experience as opposed to the employer's actual operations, the more likely the internship will be viewed as an extension of the individual's educational experience"—in other words, college credit. If, however, the intern is performing clerical work (e.g., filing, managerial duties, assisting customers), then he or she is to receive some benefits. These benefits include minimum wage and overtime requirements. This scenario requires mandatory intern pay because the employer benefits from the intern's work.

These are guidelines to keep in mind. If HR tells you that the internship is unpaid, accept or reject the offer at your expense.

+ THE PAID INTERNSHIP

An internship that offers an hourly wage is super helpful—you'll have the comfort of at least some steady, biweekly income to rely on. So you don't run into any surprises, think about the following before your internship starts.

++ TAXES

Find out what state taxes will be taken out of your paycheck. Ten dollars an hour sounds fair until the tax monster leaves you with a paycheck that needs to stretch over the next two weeks. I vividly remember looking at my internship's first paycheck and feeling absolutely robbed. But hey, at least it was something. Maybe I could order a salad with avocado next time?

++ FORMS

Ask your employer ahead of time for any financial paperwork that you need to fill out, such as a W-2 form or a copy of your personal ID. Sometimes two forms of ID will be requested—I know this because I once had to have my father scan and email my passport image for a second form of ID on my W-2. Don't mess around when it comes to payday.

++ OVERTIME

Inquire about working overtime. During one of my paid internships, the employer almost expected interns to work overtime. Early morning appointments and next-day afternoon meeting preparations called for extended time on the clock. I was averaging fifty hours a week. This was accounted for with time-and-a-half pay, as well as the occasional "Use this company credit card, Syd. Get whatever you want for breakfast."

A couple extra bucks and fewer hours to sleep. Stop it! You're too kind.

Another paid internship, however, confronted me after the first pay period. They wanted me to stay at forty hours a week because they were not prepared to pay an intern overtime wages. *Oops.* Communication is key—especially when it comes to finances. It is not a bad idea to clarify financials before your first day. You want to be on the same page as your employer, from the foreword to the index.

HOUSING

If your internship is out of state, your budget needs to take housing into account. Unfortunately, yet not surprisingly, most internships do not accommodate for housing expenses. Start by thinking about *where* exactly you plan to live during your internship. Keep in mind that internships usually last only a few months, so a year-long lease is likely out of the question.

Your best resource is the people you already know. Renting from some sort of grapevine connection gives you a sense of comfort and trust. Start by asking family members, classmates, friends, and even friends of friends of friends, and so on. I located my best housing experience through a friend of a friend. Start this networking far in advance because the more people you reach out to, the greater the chances that you'll find that someone who knows someone who could help you.

Search online for "intern housing in . . ." or "short-term student housing," and you'll have more than enough search results to get you started. If proximity to work is a crucial factor, start by searching within your internship location's zip code. Some housing sites are more trusted than others. Ask around to get some feedback before you give out any personal information.

With that in mind, here are a few housing options to consider:

- College campus dorm
- Apartment/condo
- Guest house/guest room
- Twenty-four-hour gyms (kidding, but people have told me they considered it)

TRANSPORTATION

MapQuest point A to point B.
Perfect. Only a twelve-minute commute to work.
Gets on public bus to time route to work.
Fifty minutes later.
Dammit.

If you, like me, don't want to ship a car across the country for a ten-week internship, you will need to resort to public transportation or your feet. In some cities, it's actually more convenient to get around via subway or bus system than by car. In New York City, I walked to and from work every day, and I vividly remember my anxiety the first day as I clutched my notecard of directions to help my directionally challenged self: *turn left on the corner with the flower shop*. Good thing I didn't look like a tourist (insert sarcastic emoji here).

Other cities, such as Los Angeles, are much more spread out. Most people working and living there have their own means of transportation. However, when I was in LA, I used public transportation, and I could write a book based on my Blue Bus experiences. My favorite was a man who kept yelling at the bus driver to pull over, then casually said he had a dead man in his bag. Long story short, I gained a lot of independence traveling to and from my internship by myself.

When planning out your transportation, ask yourself the following:

- Can I afford to drive to my internship from where I am living every day?
- Is public transportation an option? If so, what is the expense? Plan your transportation routes far in advance and test them out before your first day.
- Can I carpool with anyone at my internship? Ask your employer for other interns' contact information to see if this could work out.
- Do I know how to read a map? This is a serious question. Being directionally challenged is not a joke.

No matter how you transport yourself, include plenty of extra time in your plan. As you gathered from my LA bus experience,

I failed to take into account the number of stops, the passengers getting on and off, the transfers, and the psychotics transporting dead bodies.

DRESS CODE

When I say dress code, I don't actually have a rule book listing what you must wear during an internship. However, when you plan out your attire, dress for the job and dress the way you want to be addressed.

DRESS FOR THE JOB

Although it's not fair that people judge physical appearances, it happens often. An employer is going to respect you at first glance if you're dressed appropriately for the position, but not if you march into the office with an oversize frat tee and the cleanest pair of pants you found on your floor that morning. Step up your game and show that you care.

DRESS THE WAY YOU WANT TO BE ADDRESSED

Before my internships, I emailed my supervisor and asked about the company's dress code. I received answers ranging from "Don't wear heels" to "Anything!" to "We'll give you our samples to wear on days we have clients." The answers were slightly vague, but at least I knew to leave the eight pairs of heels at home.

You should be able to judge your work environment pretty easily and dress accordingly. Still, a lot of young professionals misunderstand the dos and the don'ts when it comes to dressing, especially for business-professional environments. The following covers general rules of thumb for both guys and gals to consider when dressing for an internship.

+ GUYS

Guys, I hate to break it to you, but leave at home the Sperry Top-Siders, baggy khakis, and needlepoint belt your girlfriend made you. This is the pre-real world; it's time to get serious and build your wardrobe. Dressing appropriately for your internship is not too difficult, but looks do matter in the corporate world. When I asked a very well-dressed friend of mine what he would tell a guy to wear to his internship, he said, "It's simple. Observe how other people dress in the office, but look especially to the corner offices—mirror the more successful."

Ask if your parents or grandparents can chip in while you are still able to pull the "I'm just a student!" card. Here is what you'll need, from top to bottom:

++ A WHITE OR BLUE DRESS SHIRT

Most business professionals are not fans of button-downs. You can wear a staple white or blue dress shirt time and time again. But make sure you have a way to get rid of wrinkles—know how to press the shirt yourself. There is nothing worse than wearing a nice dress shirt that looks wrinkled.

++ SOLID-COLOR TIE

There are many ways to obtain a tie on a student budget:

- How about your dad or older brother for starters?
- Check into high-end men's consignment stores.
- Buy off-season (purchase spring things in winter and vice versa) because there is a better chance that the ties will be on sale.

- Shop on eBay. Many high-quality designer ties are being sold on eBay for literally 80 percent off their retail price.

++ THE SUIT/BLAZER

You might not need to wear a suit to work every day, but if you are scheduled to sit in on an important meeting one day, you might want to step it up. When you dress too casually for a professional meeting—well, you look even more like an intern. Find a suit in a charcoal or navy color. Make sure the suit actually fits you by getting a free fitting in a men's store. It is better to wear a well-fitting cheap suit than a poorly fitting designer suit.

If a suit is financially out of the question, a navy blazer will suit just fine (pun intended). You can never go wrong with a basic navy blazer; just don't make it too frat-tastic. Again, make sure it fits well.

++ GRAY PANTS

Gray pants are a nice staple. If you are unsure what your appropriate pant size is (neither sagging below your waist nor fitting so tightly that your pant pockets stick out), then get measured.

++ A BELT

Don't look like you got dressed in the dark. It looks especially nice if your belt matches the color of your shoe leather. And don't skip any belt loops.

++ SHOES

Don't be that guy who dresses well from the waist up but hides white New Balance sneakers under the desk. Buy dark leather lace-up shoes with leather soles. And don't forget black socks! That sliver of white ankle sock showing above your shoe is a serious male faux pas.

+ GALS

As unfair as it may seem, gals have more clothing options than guys. That means finding business-professional clothing won't be a scavenger hunt—but it also means that gals have more chances to really mess things up and dress inappropriately. Keep in mind the following general staples when preparing for your internship.

++ THE WHITE BLOUSE

You can dress up or dress down this staple for any internship. It's a classic, professional piece to have.

++ NAVY BLAZER

Pair a classic navy blazer with just about anything.

++ PENCIL SKIRT

Stick to a black pencil skirt. Other colors can appear dated; plus you can pair black with anything you pack (yes, even navy). Keep it at an appropriate length (a couple inches above the knee). Look for black pencil skirts in ponte knit fabric—it's comfortable and excellent for packing because it doesn't wrinkle.

++ YOUR GO-TO FLATS

Wear heels if you so desire, but you will be much more comfortable interning in flat shoes.

+ OUT-OF-STATERS

If you're traveling out of state, take into consideration *versatility* as you pack. I had the hardest time packing for my first internship in NYC. The night before I left, I took the most versatile clothes I had, scattered them on my bed, and wrote down all of the variations of an outfit I could imagine. Sounds silly, but it worked for me. The point is to pack with a plan.

++ EXTRA ITEMS

Find out if you need to bring other toiletries. My apartment, for example, required you to bring your own towels, washcloths, soap, laundry detergent, and so on. Be proactive and save yourself from having to source these items in a new city and haul them back to where you live.

++ COMFORT IS KEY

Pack some sneakers—even if you *swear* you have the most comfortable loafers you've ever owned. A pair of Converse, obnoxiously bright Nikes, whatever—just bring them. If you will be walking (to work, on errands, running for coffee, then running for another coffee six minutes later), your feet are going to hate you after a few hours. I am convinced that there is a direct correlation between blistered feet and the most irritable mood. Just don't wear your tennies around the office.

Offices are notorious for cranking up the AC when summer's heat is at an all-time high. If you are always cold like me, pack a go-to blazer or jacket that you can wear in the office. Spending eight hours freezing in an office all day is far from ideal.

Take your commute into consideration as well. It's not okay to walk into your internship with sweat stains and body odor from your bus or subway ride that could knock out a boardroom of twelve.

+ GUYS AND GALS

Wear a watch every day. Do *not* keep your cell phone out to look at the time. You will be distracted and lose productivity. Instead, wear a watch to keep up with your schedule.

CONFIRM ALL INTERNSHIP DETAILS

One week before your internship starts, contact your mentor to confirm the location, date, and time. Some internships are set in stone so far in advance that it's easy to lose touch with your employer. This could be an issue if any changes were made (e.g., location, office hours) that your mentor failed to share with you. Since your mentor is just as busy as anybody, it is ultimately your responsibility to send an email the week before the start date to confirm the details. Let your mentor know that you are looking forward to your first day—they appreciate a jazzed-up intern who's ready for the job.

. . .

Preparation is an important part of the internship process. It is better to be overprepared than underprepared. Keep track of your internship budget, and estimate how much you have to spend on housing, transportation, food, and entertainment. Maintain communication with your employer as you prepare. Don't hesitate to ask your mentor for suggestions. Preparing for an internship can be time-consuming and tedious, but it's a journey. Enjoy it!

PREPARATION TAKEAWAYS

Budget
- Save far in advance for an unpaid internship. For a paid internship, ask your employer about taxes, financial forms, and overtime pay.

Housing
- Network with people—they're your best resource. To ensure credibility, get a second and third opinion from friends and family about housing options found online.

Transportation
- Look into the best means of traveling to and from work. Plan and test routes before your first day.

Dress Code
- Guys, gals, and out-of-staters: dress the way you want to be addressed.

Confirming the Internship
- Confirm all internship details with your employer before your first day.

THE FIRST WEEK

The real glory is being knocked to your knees and then
coming back. That's real glory. That's the essence of it.

—Vince Lombardi

I t's 9:00 a.m. It's time.

After a deep breath, I walked through the double doors
to internship day one.

Silence.

I wasn't expecting a greeting party from the high-end,
sought-after designer, but I didn't even see my mentor, who had
hired me. *No big deal, I'll just take a seat on this bench near the
showroom.*

Three gals walked in and flashed me quick smirks that said,
"Hey, intern." *Great. Am I that obvious?*

A tall, gorgeous woman with effortless brown hair stopped in
her tracks and turned to me: "Who are you?"

"I'm Sydney. I'm the new intern," I said, caught somewhat off
guard.

She paused, eyed my last-season ensemble, and said something that I will never forget: "I don't even know who hired you."
Then she moved along to greet another striking employee.

Holy . . . I sat speechless on the bench. My mental preparation
for the first week cannonballed straight down the drain. Sticks
and stones may break your bones but, damn, those words hurt.

My mind was so occupied replaying that scene that I didn't even notice my mentor walk in.

"Hi. You must be Sydney."

Insert my fake smile here.

"Hi! Yes. Sorry, I got here early, I think." I checked my watch again, acting like I didn't already know it was exactly fourteen minutes past when she had told me to arrive.

"Welcome. I'll introduce you to everyone." She quickly turned and headed into the office where smirkers one, two, and three were chatting about their fabulous weekends. I gathered my briefcase and visible insecurities, and made sure my smile was anything but a frown. Cheers to day one.

. . .

Before I scare you, I want to be up front about one thing: the first week of any internship is always the most nerve wracking and difficult. Like the first week of any job, you're dealing with a flux of mixed emotions and you don't quite know what to expect. The major difference, however, is that you are still a student, which can both benefit and hinder you. The benefit: you are not *supposed* to know everything—you are there to learn. The downside: this can hinder the amount of responsibility you are given.

Depending on the internship you have, your mentor may or may not expect you to exhibit certain skills at the start. Regardless, it is crucial to exude common sense and responsibility right off the bat. Remain positive and portray positive body language. Good or bad, effortless or awkward—first impressions just sort of *stick*.

How do you make a positive first impression, you ask? Follow these seven tips to ensure that your employer thinks highly of you from the first hello:

- There is always something to do.
- Get off your cell phone.
- Someone is always watching.
- Smile, even if you don't mean it.
- Nail the simple tasks.
- Think ahead.

COMMUNICATION IS KEY

The term *communication skills* seems simultaneously vague yet quite obvious, but I cannot reiterate enough how important it is to be up front and ask questions. *Employers would much rather have you ask questions about a task than have you complete the task incorrectly because you were unsure of yourself.*

Since you are interning *for* an employer, you need to adapt, and the only way you will adapt is by communicating thoroughly and by asking appropriate questions. When you ask questions, it shows that you are thinking ahead and that you have the courage to double-check your accuracy rather than wasting time *thinking* you can figure everything out on your own. However, make sure you ask the *right* questions to the *right* people.

My first supervisor assumed I knew how to do everything. I vividly remember asking her numerous questions whenever she gave me a task—I felt proud that she thought I knew so much, but I also felt dumb for constantly playing twenty questions. She would usually respond, "You're smart, you can figure it out." She wanted me to use resources to figure out things rather than relying on her for quick answers.

Another supervisor always told me how she was glad that I asked so many questions. *Sigh of relief.* She told me she would rather I ask tons of questions and do the task correctly than rush through a task I was unsure of and ultimately screw it up.

When in serious doubt, direct questions to your mentor or the person to whom you report. If the questions are relatively simple and can be answered by anyone in the company, ask a fellow intern first. But don't ask just any intern—ask the intern with the most common sense.

Mentoring an intern is time consuming. If your mentor typically runs low on patience, it can also be frustrating. Make mentoring you as easy on your supervisor as possible, and always try to get answers first from the resources around you.

The first week is also all about getting acquainted with the company's culture, how it operates, what its style is. It is your responsibility to introduce yourself to everyone in the office. Communicate to them who you are, why you are there, and that you are happy to meet them.

THERE IS ALWAYS SOMETHING TO DO

"What are you doing?" You'll hear this question at some point, if not many points, during your internship. Your employer could be checking in unexpectedly and asking about what you are currently working on. But if your employer is asking "What are you doing?" because you appear to have nothing to do, then you have a problem.

One afternoon, four of us interns were crowded around the front desk. One was assisting PR with media copies. One was on a lunch break, obnoxiously slurping tomato soup. I was writing out personal orders for some boutiques. And then there was a gal in the corner staring blankly at all of us who were actually doing *something*. I heard the stomping of my mentor's boots approaching the front desk. That sound came to an abrupt stop, and then I heard him backtrack. He stopped in front of the intern desk, looked around at all of us, and asked the project-less intern a question that made us feel quite uncomfortable: "Are you too important?"

"I don't think I know what you mean," she said, straightening up and suddenly realizing that she looked like an idiot just sitting there.

"You must be really important. I don't know why else you would just be sitting here when there is an entire list of things you could be doing," the supervisor said in a tone that made even me feel like I was in trouble.

The intern's face suddenly flushed white. "Uh . . . I'll work on organizing the supply closet. I'm sorry."

"I'm sorry, too." And with that, his boots took off for the exit door.

Ouch. Not exactly a pleasant encounter the first week.

Productivity levels truly set apart the good from the great interns. If you find yourself without a task to do, *find* something. Ask your employer, "Is there anything I can help you with?" Most of the time your employer will gladly pass on a task and will think highly of you for taking the initiative. Organize the supply closet, ask if anyone needs you to run an errand, make a list of goals for that week, do *something*. Utilize your time effectively and efficiently, and you'll be in good shape. Nothing looks worse than an intern sitting at a desk doing jack, or worse, on her cell phone, which brings me to my next point.

GET OFF YOUR CELL PHONE

There is a time and place for cell phone use in this technology-consumed age, but an internship is not one of them. Regardless of the people around you, and even if your mentor is often on his phone, make it a point to put away your cell phone for the day and focus on why you are there and what you want to accomplish. You will be surprised to see an immense increase in your productivity and an increase in the respect you have earned from your employers. Just because the intern next to you is Snapchatting a selfie with the caption "Intern lifeeeeee" does not mean that you should participate in the social media party as well. Act as if a potential employer is always watching you. Creepy, but wouldn't you want to always be on your best behavior? This brings me to my next point because believe it or not, someone *is* always watching.

SOMEONE IS ALWAYS WATCHING

"Sydney, can you come into our office for a minute?"

Stomach drop.

I stopped my current project—an InDesign document for the launch of the company's new social media account—and nervously entered the owners' office. My mentor turned around to my computer and smiled at my screen, which eased my nerves a tad.

"What are you using to work on that document?"

"Oh. I'm using InDesign."

"You know how to use InDesign?"

Game changer: one week later, the owners and my mentor assigned me to take over all of the entire company's social media accounts as well as to create promotional materials to be used online.

Even when you are totally unaware of it, someone is noticing your actions. If you have a strong skill set that is applicable to your internship, take a risk and exhibit those skills. Make them known by your employers in an "Oh, this ol' skill?" sort of way. This is not a suggestion about boasting and acting like you are better than everyone else. This is a lesson about highlighting your abilities in a way that can benefit the company as well as you.

Usually a person's productivity increases when they are aware that someone they want to impress is watching. Make every task one that you would feel confident doing if the owners of the company were watching you. From time management skills to organizational skills, whatever you *know* you are great at, do it even better than you did the day before. Yeah, no pressure. But setting the bar high from the start could earn you more responsibilities and respect in the long run.

On the topic of being watched, keep in mind that some companies can view activity on company computers. If you are sending emails back and forth with friends about weekend plans and how bored you are at your internship—well, bad idea. Not only could that email be flagged, but your mentor could easily tell your bored self to leave or actually get work done. When in doubt, use the company's computer with the mind-set that someone has access to what you are doing, because they very well could.

SMILE, EVEN IF YOU DON'T MEAN IT

No job is fun *all* of the time—if you find one, contact me. Remember why you are interning: to learn what you enjoy as well as what you do not particularly enjoy. The only way you will find out what you don't like to do is if you leave your personal life at the door and fully engage in the task. This sometimes means forcing a smile when you are asked to run an errand in ninety-degree heat. My initial thought, when this happened to me, was usually "Why can't the messenger do it?" as I craved responsibility and tasks that required brainwork. But I also understood that everyone begins somewhere, so my initial defense mechanism evolved into an "Of course. Need anything else while I'm out?"

"Actually, yes. I'm craving carrots and hummus."

Not what I had in mind.

Still, I proceeded with a smile because a happy mentor is a happy intern. According to an article in *Psychology Today,* "The act of smiling activates neural messaging that benefits your health and happiness. . . . Smiling activates the release of neuropeptides that work toward fighting off stress."[1]

Not only is smiling physically beneficial, but you also look better. A study done at the Face Research Laboratory at the University of Aberdeen, Scotland, found that people were more attracted to images of people who smiled than to those of people who did not smile.[2] Smiling is even contagious! Each time you flash your mentor a smile, the brain coaxes your mentor to return the favor. So go ahead—begin your internship with a pearly white smile.

NAIL THE SIMPLE TASKS

Be aware that there is no such thing as a simple task. I know employers who grade their interns on how they bring them their lunch.

Have you heard the one about the high-power executive? If he asks you to launch a space shuttle into a particular orbit and you miss a little, that's okay—it was a difficult task. If the high-power executive asks you to bring him a turkey sandwich on rye and you bring him a ham sandwich on wheat, then you've lost all trust. Why? If you can't complete a simple task correctly, you probably won't be trusted to do much else. Everything is a test, and sometimes the simplest tasks are not as easy as they seem. Nail the simple tasks to earn the opportunity for more challenging ones.

THINK AHEAD

The first week of an internship is prime time for feeling out your job and adapting. Still, even as you learn the ins and the outs of the company, think ahead and anticipate. If you know that an important client is coming into the office the next day, ask if there is anything you can do to help prepare. If your company has weekly meetings, prepare a list of questions as well as a recap of what you have been working on. Being prepared will impress your employer, and it will also make you appear smarter and more creative. It shows that you are making an effort. All of that can lead to more opportunities. Although it is important to focus on the present, it is also beneficial to take time to organize and prepare yourself for what's to come.

. . .

The first week of an internship is truly exciting if you allow it to be. No matter what's on your to-do list, it's up to you to be the best version of yourself—you're representing the company and also your future in the industry. We all have ups and downs. Trust me—I'm familiar with these roller-coaster thoughts. When you focus on why you are there, when you are grateful for the experience, and when you turn every mistake into a lesson learned—*that* is when you see the open road for growth. Ultimately the only limits you face are the limits you put on yourself. The worst mistake you can possibly make during your first week is not to take full advantage of the internship. This is your time to contribute, be an example for other interns, and set the bar. What do you have to lose?

THE FIRST WEEK TAKEAWAYS

Communication Is Key
- Always ask questions—don't assume the answers.

There Is Always Something to Do
- Don't just sit there. *Do* something.

Get Off Your Cell Phone
- Just because your mentor is texting (or Snapchatting, Facebooking, or Instagramming) doesn't mean you should be.

Someone Is Always Watching
- Always perform like your boss is standing over your shoulder.

Smile, Even If You Don't Mean It
- No one likes a sour face. It's unprofessional, unnecessary, and ugly.

Nail the Simple Tasks
- Get the simple tasks right to prove your capabilities.

Think Ahead
- Anticipate what needs to be done, strategize, and plan ahead.

THE STEREOTYPICAL INTERN

It ain't what they call you. It's what you answer to.
—W. C. Fields

P icture this. It's the first week of your first internship in New York City. Your only goal for the week is to not look stupid or get in the way. A PR staffer stops you and asks if you could run and grab her a coffee. You force a smile and say you would be happy to. You take note of her request for the shade of brown she wants. You grab your cell phone, then you make your way down West Thirty-Seventh.

How hard could it be? Pretty damn hard, given that you realize you didn't ask if she wanted iced or hot. You think you should wing it and get an iced—it's humid today, after all—but you stop yourself to call the office. Hot. She wants hot.

This exact scenario happened to me three summers ago. The cliché coffee run. A coffee run may feel belittling, but only if you make it out to be. Whatever you have to do, it is up to you to pull that energy out of the air and prove to your employer that you are not the cliché. Prove you are capable of anything, from the most tedious task to the most challenging project. All tasks will build, if not your skill sets, then at least your character: If it hadn't been for my countless errands, including one where I was sent out three times because each time I brought back the client the *wrong* Greek yogurt (there is a huge difference between peach and pineapple—okay, I get it), then I would not have the self-reliance and capabilities that I have today.

As an intern, you will be faced with stereotypes—such as scampering the city on coffee runs, performing mundane tasks, and slumming it at the bottom of the corporate totem pole. If you find yourself stuck in a stereotype, read on to find how to break out of it and get the most out of your situation.

MYTH: INTERNS DO WHAT NO ONE ELSE WANTS TO DO

It's common to think of an intern as the person to pick up the tasks that no one really likes to do, such as the endless errand runners—jotting down drink orders, triple-checking that they haven't lost the company credit card, and constantly eyeing their watch so they return to the office at a reasonable time. Or the constant mundane task-doer—printing notes, filing last season's client orders, and stapling employee handbooks. The stereotype isn't that you *won't* be doing these things—because you very well could be. The stereotype is that this is *all* you do or are capable of doing as an intern. Don't think of these tasks as ones that no one else wants to do; think of them as tasks assigned to you because you can do them *better* than the rest. Read on to learn how to turn negative stereotypes into positive opportunities.

+ CONQUER THE ERRANDS

Running errands is not a punishment, even if it might feel like it. If that job description sounds like yours, don't despair. Look at running errands as an opportunity to show your employer just how much of an asset you can be. Keep your head high, accept the task with a smile, and run those errands better than any intern they've ever had. Plus, think of the awesome exercise you'll get instead of sitting in a chair with bad posture, straining your eyes at a computer screen, and keyboarding for hours on end.

Think about a CEO you greatly respect. Chances are that CEO began in a position like yours. Bill Gates, for example, spent his high school junior year in Washington, D.C., as a congressional page. He did administrative tasks, prepared the House chambers, and delivered messages—probably more deliveries than he wanted. Although errands can feel repetitive and sometimes unnecessary, someone has to do them. So conquer them and do them well. Employers will pick up on the interns who gladly accept the far-from-glamorous tasks without complaint.

+ BE A TEAM PLAYER

One summer Friday afternoon at my marketing internship in LA, I was so ready for the weekend, being with friends, and sleeping in past 6:00 a.m. This particular afternoon, however, consisted of checking shipments of hundreds (literally) of boxes with next season's inventory. Given the small size of the company, everyone was called to help assist in taking inventory, counting each item in each box, as well as taking note of the items' sizes to make sure that the manufacturer didn't accidentally forget one size-small shirt. Tedious? To say the least. But I put all my energy into the task and enjoyed the fast-paced, busy afternoon. Turns out the vice president of sales then told the owners how he admired my ability to pick up on any task and errand that was asked of me, without "huffing and puffing negativity," as he put it. He respected my humility and my ability to be a part of the team, no matter the task at hand.

+ YOU NEVER KNOW UNTIL YOU ASK

Sometimes you might take an internship without knowing exactly what you will be doing. Before one of my sales internships, I asked my mentor for a list of specific responsibilities and tasks that would be expected of me during the summer. I told her that I wanted a lot of responsibility because I enjoy challenges. She promised me that I would have very specific day-to-day responsibilities, as well as my own desk, phone line, and email. Quite official for an intern! I was pumped. Despite her promise, I was faced with more errands in a day than a UPS delivery truck on Christmas Eve.

Sound familiar? It may feel totally out of your comfort zone to ask for more responsibilities, but once you feel you've proven yourself as a capable errand runner and team player, don't be afraid to ask for more challenging tasks. It was out of my comfort zone, too, but I gave it a shot anyway after a week. My supervisor acknowledged and appreciated my request but informed me that the week's back-to-back appointments called for coffee runs for clients. She did, however, assure me that next week's tasks would bring more of a challenge. Because I showed initiative and openness by asking for more responsibilities, and knowing that challenges were in store, I was able to enjoy the internship more. So don't be let down when you find yourself with a company AmEx and a list of beverage orders. In the end, you'll be one of the most liked in the office. Why? Because you are delivering their caffeine, that's why.

MYTH: THE OFFICE PHONE IS TERRIFYING

There is nothing quite like answering the office phone for the first time, especially when you're told that interns must pick up the phone before the second ring. I doubt your mentor will set aside time to teach you how to not be an idiot on the phone, so follow these phone etiquette tips to avoid tripping up and making your coworkers mad.

+ TRANSFERRING

Don't sweat when it comes to figuring out what to say when you answer the phone. Just mimic what the rest of the office says. However, when it comes to transferring a call, office phones vary greatly. Ask the other interns how to transfer a call if you don't already know how.

Beyond how to press the buttons, it's important to know when and when not to transfer. Some employees are insistent on answering every call right away. Others would rather have you take a message if they're caught in the middle of something else. Then there are the employees who hear a client's name and do all they can to avoid the call.

+ TAKING MESSAGES

I hate to burst your bubble, but you are going to make a mistake at least once when it comes to the office phone. My first internship's big "oopsie" moment happened one Friday afternoon. We were celebrating the senior designer's birthday with Japanese food. (Yes, I ran that errand and picked up a decadent cake from the bakery around the corner.) The entire office was in a good mood because of the excused eating and socializing. In the midst of the cake cutting, the phone rang. I looked around the room. No one budged. The second ring was just a few seconds away. I ran to the front desk to pick up the phone. The person on the other line happened to be the CEO. She asked if so-and-so was available. Naturally, my instincts told me to answer honestly.

"She's actually just now cutting her birthday cake!" I said happily.

A few really long seconds of silence later, the CEO replied, "You guys are celebrating without me?"

Way to go, Sydney.

The office welcomed me back to the celebration by asking about the phone call, and the celebration came to an abrupt halt. Let's just say that an office celebration without the CEO was a red flag. After an awkward silence, a decrease in my intern brownie points, and my sincere apologies, I answered the phone much differently from then on. That phone call quickly taught me to think ahead (and to take messages during CEO-less office birthday celebrations).

Here's a tip about taking messages: if you answer the phone and have to take a message, blame it on a meeting when in doubt. Here are examples:

- The head of marketing is not on vacation; he is just *unavailable at the present time.*
- The CEO is not taking her kid to soccer practice; she is just *in a meeting.*
- The vice president of sales is not out for lunch; she is *on a conference call.*

Catch my drift? It is unprofessional to tell the person on the other line that so-and-so is on a lunch break. After all, you don't want to make it sound like someone is out, meandering, and not doing their job. Write down a detailed message and deliver it when the person returns. Answering the phone is not for conversing—it is for taking a message and then relaying it.

If the recipient's phone line is busy, write down the name of the person and what they are calling about. Slide that piece of paper onto the desk of the person you are trying to reach. They will either tell you to take a message, scribble in all caps "NO WAY. HE'S CRAZY!" (happened to me), or take the call. Again, don't assume—always ask.

MYTH: INTERNSHIPS GRANT YOU A JOB

Students are continuously searching for ways to make themselves look awesome on paper. They join clubs, volunteer, study ruthlessly to earn good (or passing) grades, and work internships. Although these activities are great, they won't guarantee that you will get your dream job, but they *could* get you closer to it. Understand that even if you were merely the coffee gopher at Goldman Sachs, the ability to put the company's name on your résumé adds some credibility. Internships not only look good on a résumé, but they also increase your chances of landing your dream job because of your experiences. Of course, job security is not guaranteed.

MYTH: INTERNS WILL ALWAYS BE AT THE BOTTOM OF THE TOTEM POLE

The question is not if you will be on the bottom of the totem pole but *what you will do* to get noticed in a positive way. What capabilities will you demonstrate to prove to your employer that you have the abilities to exceed what is expected of the lower tier? Start proving yourself on day one.

Many people initially think interns are young and unfamiliar with the company's work environment, so they place them at the bottom of the office hierarchy. While this may be true, it does not have to define what *you* do. Xerox CEO Ursula Burns began at the bottom of the ladder as an intern. Her breakthrough of the invisible intern barrier came largely from her mother's advice: "*Where* you are is not *who* you are."

Go into an internship knowing that you won't be discouraged if the tasks you are required to perform are not always what you hoped for. If you have the mind-set of a kick-ass employee, chances are you'll be treated like one. Your capacity to do great work during your internship is primarily based on how you perceive yourself. If you view yourself as worthy of only the bottom rung, then you will stay there.

With that said, you have to prove yourself. Before I wrote this book, I created a questionnaire to give to students, graduates, and friends in a multitude of industries, all of whom had completed at least one internship. One of my questions was, "What do you wish you had done differently during your internship?" Out of all the questions I asked, this one received the most similar responses: "I wish I could have been more outgoing." The core of this response is that interns sometimes don't think they are *allowed* to be outgoing and opinionated. They don't realize until after the internship that they could have improved their position in the organization.

To break out of the mold, ask yourself, "What value will I add as an intern?"

. . .

Stereotypes are simply characteristics that describe the majority of a group; there are always exceptions, however. I encourage you to acknowledge that you will likely run into these stereotypes. Prepare yourself for these preconceptions with determination to perform better than the expected norm.

"Stereotypes do exist, but we have to walk through them."
—Forest Whitaker

THE STEREOTYPICAL
INTERN TAKEAWAYS

"Interns do what no one else wants to do."
- As an intern you might be stuck with performing mundane tasks, so perform the tasks better than any other intern. Don't think of them as tasks others don't want to do—think of them as a starting point.

"The office phone is terrifying."
- Think ahead when answering the phone and take detailed messages.

"Internships grant you a job."
- Don't assume that you will receive a job offer after an internship. Instead, intern to see if you would potentially want to work there.

"Interns will always be at the bottom of the totem pole."
- Remember that your title as "intern" is not permanent. Everyone starts somewhere, but it's up to you to aim for the top or remain at the bottom.

THE STANDOUT INTERN

Either you run the day, or the day runs you.
—Jim Rohn

Society always wants more. More money, more clothes, more cars, more gadgets . . . the list goes on. Theoretically, we can get more money. We can also get more *things* once we have more money. There is one thing, however, that we cannot get more of: time.

Time is incredibly valuable. The most successful people in this world don't have more hours in a day than anybody else. It's how they spend their hours that makes all the difference. You may have heard the saying "You have the same amount of hours in a day as Beyoncé." Although this trending saying is technically true, a recent study in the *Journal of Experimental Social Psychology* challenges its meaning. According to the study, "Power increases perceptions of available time, and that perceived control over time underlies this effect." People who viewed themselves as higher up on the organizational ladder—for example, a CEO—felt that they had more available time than people who were lower on that ladder. This occurs because powerful people have the ability to alter their schedule—such as cancel a meeting—for their convenience.[1]

What about an intern's valuable time? Some will argue that interns are *below* the bottom of the ladder because they are not even considered employees. Because of this belittling placement, interns tend to feel that there is not enough time in the day to create the impact they desire. In reality, that's just not the case. Although interns cannot cancel meetings, assign someone else to run their errands, or conveniently show up late to a meeting, interns do have control of their actions and how they allot their time.

Looking back on my first coffee run mishap, I realize my misuse of time. Instead of calling the office to ask if Miss Priss wanted a hot or cold coffee, the best decision I could have made was to purchase both. I would have shown up prepared, I would have solved a problem on my own rather than dialing SOS, and I would have saved time—time that you can never get back.

As an intern, you are given responsibilities and tasks, as well as a timeline for completing them. The difference between an average and a standout intern is the drive to complete tasks before deadlines and to always go above and beyond. To do this, you must learn to be a strong self-manager.

THE SELF-MANAGER

Although an internship is designed to be a learning experience, your mentor is not there to babysit you. Still, teaching an intern the ins and outs of a typical workday can take up a lot of time and energy—your mentor has to take time to ensure that you understand your responsibilities and what is expected of you. Respect your mentor's limited time by going into the internship with the ability to manage yourself. In other words, practice self-management.

Self-management forces you to think of yourself as a top-notch, valuable employee. A recent study highlights the importance of self-management.

What exactly is self-management? According to Valikhani and Karimi, it is "controlling and dominating your thoughts, affects, behavior, performance, and events. [It] derives from social knowledge."[2] Conducting such control from the start of your internship will greatly benefit you. As with most self-management practices, you must follow a process. The following list includes some of what I agree are the most important steps in the process of self-management:

- Set goals.
- Prioritize goals.
- Organize.
- Achieve satisfaction.
- Be accountable.
- Concentrate.

+ SET GOALS—COMPARE GOALS BEFORE YOUR INTERNSHIP TO NOW

In "The Search" section of this book, I explained the purpose and benefits of writing down personal internship goals. Refer to your list of goals, and write down how your current intern tasks relate to those goals or how you can tangibly achieve those goals before the end of your internship. The act of comparing your goals from before your internship to your most recent tasks will put into perspective where you are with your goals and what you need to do to reach them.

+ PRIORITIZE GOALS—DO THE HARDEST THING FIRST

I'll be the first one to admit that I struggle to prioritize goals. I constantly find myself working on small, hardly meaningful tasks that at the time make me feel productive but require the smallest amount of energy. The book *Eat That Frog!* by Brian Tracy really taught me the importance of completing the biggest, most difficult task first. The book introduces twenty-one ways to get more done in less time, and its lessons are relevant to tasks you'll be assigned during your internship.

At the beginning of my last internship, I was assigned to develop a company's social responsibility plan. From the strategy to the action plan, a lot of parts went into researching and developing it. The project as a whole looked to me like one morbidly obese frog I was going to have to swallow (yuck).

I had nine weeks to develop and present the program to the owners. To ensure that I would have enough time, I developed specific goals to meet by the end of each week. This helped me visualize how long I would need to work on each part. My weekly written goals also helped me prioritize what goal needed to be met first, second, and so on. Every other week I scheduled a time to meet with the owners to show them my progress, which was an important goal of mine. I wanted to ensure that we were all on the same page. Nothing is worse than spending hours of your time working on something and then your boss says, "Nah, not what I had in mind. Try again." Ugh, the worst.

To prioritize, ask three questions:

- What is most important?
- How long do I expect the project to take?
- When are specific tasks due/when should certain goals be met?

Asking your mentor for deadlines will help you prioritize and understand what your mentor values, what will be important in the near future, and what you should do if you have spare time. Don't be surprised if you find that you need to reevaluate your priorities as you continue to work. For example, I underestimated the amount of time it would take for me to research social responsibility programs, how they're established, and all of the different parts that make up each program. I soon realized that I needed to make my research goals a higher priority.

Being able to prioritize your goals is a crucial part of the self-management process. Remember, time is indispensible. As Brian Tracy explains in his book, find the biggest frog and tackle it first and foremost when you have most of your energy. At the end of the day, you'll be glad you did.

+ ORGANIZE—STRATEGICALLY AND EFFECTIVELY

I have always been meticulously organized. Growing up, I color coordinated my closet, my desk drawer looked like a display in the Container Store, and my backpack's books were in order from first period to sixth. Today, my friends joke that my daily planner would give them an anxiety attack from all of my personal notes and to-dos, but I assure them that it's just how I function. When it comes to organizing goals, I'm not saying you should color code and alphabetize your list, but you *should* discover a way to organize your goals and tasks in a way that works best for you.

If your internship is similar to my last one, you will be balancing a lot at once. I had to keep track of weekly meetings, daily social media posts, blog content, social responsibility updates, and upcoming email blasts, to name a few of my responsibilities. Sometimes I had to step outside to get some fresh air when my to-do list was hanging over my head like a storm cloud. To keep my anxiety from skyrocketing, I would return to my desk, take some deep breaths, and organize. At the beginning of the week, I would perform the following routine to help me stay on track:

- Look ahead.
- Check to see when meetings that I needed to prepare for were scheduled.
- Tackle daily and weekly goals.
- Write the social media content I planned to post for that week, getting together all images and text for each account and saving everything in separate labeled folders.
- Develop an outline for that week's blog content.
- Tackle long-term goals.
- Dedicate an hour to research and development of the social responsibility plan.
- Completely dedicate an hour to potential blog partnerships and communicating with bloggers.
- Remember to breathe, smile, and take advantage of half-off Starbucks from 2:00 to 4:00 p.m.

Without an organized routine, it would have been very difficult for me to get everything done in a single day. Once you understand all of your responsibilities and roughly how long it takes you to complete the related tasks, organize yourself both physically and mentally.

Physical organization means cleaning off your desk, writing down anything you think you could forget, planning ahead, and being thorough.

Mental organization means focusing on your written goals and priorities.

Your mentor will notice your above-average ability to organize because you'll be completing tasks effectively and very well.

No doubt you'll stand out compared to the intern who's tweeting "So much to do, so little time. #InternProbz." Enough tweeting about things you can control. Plan strategically, organize effectively, and—seriously—don't forget about the Starbucks happy hour.

+ ACHIEVE SATISFACTION—CELEBRATE EFFORTS

The feeling of true satisfaction is a direct result of hard work. If you feel unfulfilled in your internship, ask yourself if you worked hard enough to achieve the goals that you've prioritized and organized. Once you reach your goals, throw yourself a small celebration. Cave in on that ice cream shop you've passed every day for the past month. Splurge on a new outfit that you can wear to your internship next Monday. Or simply congratulate yourself and write about how proud you are of your achievement. For example, during my first internship I told myself that I deserved a new dress to wear to work if I did one thing a day for one week that was out of my comfort zone. Every night I would write down that one scary thing I did and what I learned from it. At the end of the week, I purchased a dress from the in-house designer with my intern discount and felt that I really earned it. Positive reinforcements can act as encouragement during your self-management process, so go ahead—celebrate!

+ BE ACCOUNTABLE—IT'S NOT THEM, IT'S YOU

All of my mentors absolutely hated one thing: excuses.

Stay away from excuses. It doesn't look good when you make a mistake and blame the employee who has been working at the company for the past three years.

Excuses are merely ways people conduct blame to someone or something else instead of holding themselves accountable. Standout interns accept their mistakes, acknowledge where they went wrong, and move on with more wisdom than they previously had. One of the most important processes of self-management is learning to be accountable for your actions. An intern who owns up to a mistake is much more admirable than an intern who makes an excuse for it.

I once reached out to a successful financial adviser who had a lot of experience managing interns. He told me that one of the biggest issues he has with interns happens to be excuse making. I asked him to tell me about a time that an intern refused to acknowledge accountability. He told me about asking an intern to email him a spreadsheet, but the intern printed the spreadsheet and put it on his desk. He asked the intern why she hadn't listened. A standout intern would have responded, "I have no excuse. I promise not to let it happen again. I will email the spreadsheet to you right away." Instead, his intern replied, "I didn't hear you say that." Not only did his intern make an excuse, but she also admitted that she didn't listen—double mistake.

+ CONCENTRATE—EYE ON THE PRIZE

I'm sure you have heard the quote "What you think you become." Or maybe you know the famous Henry Ford quote: "If you think you can do a thing or think you can't do a thing, you're right." These sayings are true. The mind is so powerful that it can control our actions. It's literally mind over matter.

Many factors go into a person's ability to concentrate, such as sleep, nutrition, and overall energy level. Your first internship might be the first time you experience forty-hour workweeks. Some days you will want to throw your iced coffee at the next person who speaks to you. We all have those days. Even when stress levels rise, errands accumulate, and money is scarce, we are still in control of our minds. Focus on what you are gaining from the internship. Don't focus on the unimportant things. Like the caller who got under your skin. Think big picture.

Focus your time and energy on your goals, starting with your first priority, and dedicate all of your attention to that goal. Take breaks every now and then to maintain clarity, continue to visualize your goals, and concentrate on the results. Keep your eye on the prize.

. . .

This pre-real world is your chance to exercise your mind and skill set in ways that you may not have done before. Remember to value your time and that of others because it's a limited quantity. Practice self-management, as it will help you be a standout during your internship and beyond.

A great friend of mine told me something that has forever changed the way I perform in every aspect of life. He said, "Society continuously overpromises and underdelivers. Once you learn to underpromise and overdeliver, you'll always stand out."

THE STANDOUT
INTERN TAKEAWAYS

- Be a self-manager:
- Set goals.
- What do you want from an internship? Write it down!
- Prioritize goals.
- Complete the most difficult and time-consuming goal/task first.
- Organize.
- Keep track of prioritized goals.
- Achieve satisfaction.
- Celebrate even your small achievements.
- Be accountable.
- Leave your excuses at the door.
- Concentrate.
- Devote your energy to one task at a time.

THE LAST WEEK

A ship in a harbor is safe, but
that's not what ships are built for.
—William G. T. Shedd

S ometimes you just *really* don't feel like going to a lecture. Especially one that isn't mandatory.

Shane was a performance nutrition intern who worked closely with professional athletes, dietitians, strength and conditioning specialists, chefs—the whole nine yards. During his internship, his mentor highly recommended that he attend all of the lectures provided to the facility's interns. Although the lectures were optional, Shane made it a point to go to every single one. He learned about industry trends and different types of training, and he heard advice from high-profile coaches. Then, during the last lecture, something changed his entire internship experience.

This particular lecture provided resources for moving on after the internship—how to finalize résumés for potential employers, network, and apply for a job in this particular industry. At the end of the lecture, the speaker announced that everyone there would receive a one-on-one evaluation with one of the coaches (sort of like how a professor will give bonus points to the people who come to a low-attendance class).

Nervous yet excited, Shane was paired with a coach with whom he had worked closely during his internship. The coach was one of those guys whose voice was always louder than necessary, no matter the circumstance, but it certainly always captured Shane's attention. At their meeting, the coach slid a piece of paper in front of Shane. Shane's eyes fell toward the paper and then back up at the coach.

"You're welcome," the coach said to break the silence.

"What is this?" Shane asked, quickly glancing over the document to figure out what it was.

"It's a promise from me to you. If you ever need a letter of recommendation, I can provide one for you. Why? Because you not only showed up to the last lecture, but you also showed up to every lecture, and that doesn't go unnoticed. You utilize opportunities, so I've got you covered."

Shane tried hard to subdue his excitement. "Thank you so much! I will definitely take you up on that. I've really enjoyed my internship here."

"Good, glad to hear it. Now that we've got the good news put aside, let's talk about where you can improve."

Shane's nerves picked up again, but he was prepared to improve.

That one-on-one meeting was the most beneficial part of Shane's internship. If he hadn't gone the extra mile and taken advantage of his resources, he would not have received a personalized letter of recommendation or honest feedback on how to improve—all of which made his last week a strong end to his interning experience.

. . .

"It's over already?"

I found myself asking that question at the end of every internship. After all of the early morning alarms, bottomless cups of much-needed caffeine, nerve-wracking meetings with my mentor, and continuous mental assurance that I wasn't completely messing up, the roller-coaster journey would come to an abrupt stop.

Picture yourself leaving your internship on your last day. Did you enjoy the experience to its fullest? Or did you perform timidly and continuously check your safety net in fear for your life? Let's hope you can leave the office for the last time feeling like you took a risk, even if at times you were scared. For me, the scariest part of the last week is leaving with regrets. Because of this fear, I constantly remind myself that I would rather say "At least I tried" than regret saying "I wish I would have."

The constant coming and going of eager-to-learn students can be overwhelming for an organization and your mentor. Ask yourself, "How will I be remembered?" Read on to learn how to end your internship on a high note and ensure that you won't be forgotten. Remember when I told you to think about what one thing you will contribute to the company that is unique to you? This is the time to prove that your contribution was a success.

THE WRAP-UP

The last week of your internship is actually the most crucial time to stay focused and work toward leaving an awesome and lasting impression on your employers. At this point, you will be familiar with the company environment, your daily responsibilities, and what is expected of you. Now it's up to you to wrap up everything you've been working on, instead of carelessly leaving projects incomplete. Trust me: no one wants to clean up an intern's unfinished work.

At my last internship, I managed the company's Twitter, Facebook, Instagram, Google+, Pinterest, and blog accounts, and

I used similar language, photo filters, and fonts across all of the platforms to create a unified and recognizable brand presence. I built upon our following and created a system for when I would post, what I would post, and how I would comment on our loyal followers' accounts. It felt great to make a noticeable difference within the company. The catch? I wondered what would happen to the accounts when I left. I felt connected to this brand and considered it my responsibility to make sure it was left in good hands. So, I began the wrap-up.

The wrap-up involves tying up any loose ends during the last few days of your internship. The easiest way to successfully wrap up your internship is to put yourself in your mentor's shoes. Ask yourself, "If I had an intern, what could they do that would make my job easier?" You might complete an Excel spreadsheet for your mentor's client, or make a list of projects that you wanted to do but didn't get around to. In my case, I made sure that the social media accounts would be kept in sync by creating a list of every social media account. Next to each account, I listed its characteristics and any specifics that might help the next social media manager. Although my mentor didn't ask for this summarized list, I can assure you she was impressed (aka brownie points). If you can manage your last week in a way that will take a load off your mentor's never-ending to-do list, you'll be a step ahead of the game.

THE FEEDBACK

If you're interning for school credit, your professor may already have an evaluation form for your mentor to fill out. The downfall? You don't get to read it! It's meant to be confidential. What's the point of having your mentor evaluate you if you don't get to read it? If your internship isn't for school credit, there may be no evaluation at all. Either way, it's up to you to ask for feedback.

Feedback will help you understand what you could have done differently and how to improve.

Tell your mentor that you truly value his or her opinion and that you'd like to be evaluated before the end of your internship. Doing so will communicate that you took your position seriously and that you are eager to learn and improve.

There is a right way and a wrong way to ask for feedback. The right way is to go into the conversation with a list of questions to ask your mentor, such as the following:

- What was my greatest weakness as an intern?
- What was my greatest strength?
- What did I improve on most during my internship?
- What could I have done differently to make your job easier?
- On a scale of 1 to 10, how did I rank as an intern for this company? If I wasn't a 10, what should I do to perform like a 10?

If you want to really make a positive impression, take it upon yourself to compose an evaluation form for your employer to fill out—even if your internship isn't for school credit.

Reach out to your mentor at the beginning of your last week to plan the best time for your evaluation. Your mentor might want you to email your questions in advance. If your mentor takes the evaluation a bit more personally and wants to set up a time to talk in person, you will want to bring your prewritten questions with you to the meeting. Also bring along a notebook, a pen, and topics of conversation or concerns you have regarding the internship. And bring an appetite for improvement. Receiving feedback can be nerve wracking. Here are three things to consider before your feedback meeting:

Remember not to get upset if your mentor gives you constructive criticism. Take this criticism as opportunity to improve. If you are never criticized for anything, you won't know how to alter your thinking and performance.

Remember that feedback is valuable. If I stopped writing this book at the first constructive comment I received, let's just say I wouldn't have made it far enough to "Save As" my first document. Honest feedback can sometimes feel harsh, but it is fuel for improvement.

Remember that you get to choose from whom you take advice. Everyone can speak his or her mind, but not every opinion is worth taking. Go with your gut. If you know you worked as hard as you could and sense that the criticism is unfounded, then ignore it! Choose wisely, choose intelligently, and apply worthy criticism appropriately.

THE HANDWRITTEN NOTE

My parents engrained deep in my mind the importance of handwritten letters. As inboxes fill, text messages *ding*, and phone conversations echo through our ears, it's no wonder that we look forward to a handwritten note every now and then. An email takes minutes to send, a text takes seconds to type, and a verbal "Thank you" is easily lost among other conversations. It takes time and thought to compose a handwritten thank-you note, and that doesn't go unnoticed.

Even before I met my supervisors, I wanted them to know that I was thankful for the internship opportunities. Some may call that a suck-up move, but I can assure you that was never my intention. Instead, I believe that an employer's final impression of you is even more important than a first, potentially judgmental, impression.

When you write the note, there's no need to be cheesy. Don't thank your mentor for "helping make your dreams come true" or some other bull. Instead, write a simple reflection on what you learned from the company and specifically from your mentor. That alone goes a long way. Even just four sentences can leave a lasting impression. Here's an example:

> *Dear Liz:*
>
> *I cannot believe it's already my last week! Thank you so much for the opportunity this summer to intern. You were an incredible mentor, and I really respected how you treated me like an employee from day one. Thank you again for all you taught me and encouraged me to do.*
>
> *All the best,*
> *Sydney*

Don't leave an internship with a cold and unappreciative attitude—that could cost you a lot. Keep in mind that even if the relationship wasn't exactly perfect, your mentor may know someone, who knows someone, who knows someone else, and that last someone could be the person that you work for someday. Yep. Don't want to mess that one up. People talk, especially within similar industries. Take the high road, the extra five minutes it'll take you to write the note, and hand deliver that missive. You'll be glad you did.

THE NETWORK LIST

What exactly is a network list? It is a list of people to keep track of for now and the future. They might be professionals in your desired industry, such as your mentor. They might also be people who just know a lot of people you might want to contact.

Before you leave your internship, be sure to take note of the name, number, email address, and so on of anyone in the office with whom you want to keep in touch. Start this list in a file titled something like "Networks" so you can easily find and edit it. Add the following information for every person on your network list:

- Name
- Email
- Phone (usually the office phone)
- Company name
- Position in the company
- Date you met them/worked for them
- How you can benefit them/how they can benefit you
- Anything else you might find useful

Keeping track of your networking contacts from your internship will pay off in the long run. Whenever you need endorsements or recommendations, this list will be your best friend. I applied for a marketing and business internship in New York City before my junior year of college and was so hooked on getting it that I had my past mentor create a letter of recommendation specifically for this internship application, although it wasn't required or even recommended. I landed the internship! I don't know if the letter was the main reason why, but it sure didn't hurt.

THE LAST CALL

If you get to the last week of your internship and realize that you haven't taken any risks, now is your chance. The number-one thing I think of when I think of taking risks is *awkward*, so hopefully you've experienced multiple awkward, risky moments during your internship. Why? Because most comfort zones are expanded through awkward situations and discomfort. When I went out of my comfort zone during my first internship to take one last risk, it ended up being incredibly awkward—but worth it in the end.

At my first internship, the sales rep invited me to sit in on a few merchandise meetings. The critiques, suggestions, opinions, and dramatic comments I heard were music to my ears. As my last meeting approached, I decided I would step up and project my own opinion. After all, I felt that I had good taste and a reasonably worthy opinion, and could formulate suggestions that might be of value. I brought my own notebook and pen to the meeting and took notes on the designers' presentation. After the last garment was shown, the presenter asked, "Thoughts?" After the vice president of the company shared her opinion, I had an urge to speak my mind: "I think the pattern is youthful, but the fit is older. It seems unbalanced, and the customer might be confused."

Suddenly, all eyes were on me. You would have thought I had yelled, "That's the ugliest thing I've ever seen!" Seriously, the stares burned.

"Thank you, Sydney, but I think we're looking to hear comments from everyone else," one of the designers said.

I nodded, cheeks turning bright red, and the vice president continued. The meeting went on as if I hadn't said a word. After the meeting ended, I confronted the sales rep and asked her if making a suggestion in the meeting had been wrong. She replied, "Your suggestion wasn't wrong. It just wasn't your place." *Awkward.*

Ironically, the design team cut that style from the line a few months later, and it was never manufactured. Although my suggestion was disregarded, I believe that stepping out of my comfort zone allowed me to leave a lasting impression on the design team and the other employees in the meeting. Of course I felt awkward and embarrassed, but in the end I spoke my mind and showed the company that I was not afraid to voice my opinion. Whether that gets accepted or rejected is up to them, but fortunately I could leave saying "At least I tried."

The impact of your internship—whether you leave with more networks, opportunities, advice, and experience than you thought possible, or not—is entirely up to you, but you have to intentionally seek out what you want.

Your last week is your last call to ask the questions you've been wanting to ask. Your last call to tell your mentor that you would do anything to work for this company after graduation. And your last call to thank the owners for giving you this opportunity. Don't forget to get the contact information of anyone with whom you want to stay in touch postinternship (networking!). Although this can be easier said than done, the more you practice going out of your comfort zone, the greater your zone will expand and the easier it will get.

. . .

An actor friend of mine in LA recently gave me a great piece of advice: "People continuously tell you that you have time. Time to do things you haven't done, time to figure things out, and time to tell people things you've always wanted to say. Before you know it, a year has gone by. Then another five. Then you're fifty years old and hiring a life coach because you've done all you can to get back on track." Moral of the story: time flies, so don't leave your internship with bottled regrets. Think ahead, work hard, continue to work hard, and take risks. Walk out of those office doors on your last day with a smile on your face and the ability to tell yourself "I did it." Remember: "Everything you've ever wanted is on the other side of fear" (George Addair).

THE LAST WEEK TAKEAWAYS

The Wrap-up
- Wrap up everything you have been working on and make life easy on your mentor.

The Feedback
- Discuss evaluation options with your mentor.

The Handwritten Note
- A handwritten thank-you note goes a long way.

The Network List
- Make a list of the names and contact information of people in the office with whom you want to keep in touch.

The Last Call
- Think back on your internship and tackle anything you've been wanting to do. Leave without regrets!

THE FOLLOW-UP

You already know everyone you need to know.

—Bob Beaudine

Three months after my first internship I was back in New York City for a business trip. Just a sophomore in college, I was still totally awestruck by the jam-packed streets, excessive honking, and skyscrapers that went on for miles. It felt good to be back. One afternoon, a coworker and I had some leisure time, so I told her I wanted to surprise the office staff where I'd interned. Our hotel was within walking distance. After my coworker's approval, I anxiously headed in that direction.

Is this a good idea? I thought to myself. Surprising my mentor and other employees in the middle of a workday could either be a pleasant surprise or an unwanted interruption. I listened to my gut and decided that a surprise visit couldn't hurt.

When I got there, I looked up at the building I had walked in and out of a hundred times. Only three months ago I had been living the life of a fashion intern. Time flies. I courageously walked into the lobby, where Steve, the lobby guy, always greeted me. He was still there. Out of habit, Steve smiled at me and said, "Hello, ma'am. Welcome!" Then he realized who I was and added, "Sydney, you're back! We've missed you!" His optimism was contagious. Everyone liked Steve.

"I missed being here!" I said. "Just visiting. I'll only be a few minutes."

He hit the "Up" button for me, stepped into the elevator, pressed level four, and held the door open for me as he stepped out. I wasn't even surprised that he remembered my floor. I smiled and thanked him. Once the doors closed, my plastered smile quickly faded into a lip-biting, wide-eyed stare. I was so nervous. They always say nerves are a good thing—it means you actually care.

Floor four seemed to arrive much faster than it used to when I was T minus one minute away from being late. I collected myself and walked down the long hall to the main office door. Inside, I turned to my left, where I knew the interns would be.

"Hi. My name is Sydney Fulkerson. I'm here to see Kevin."

Suddenly, I was having flashbacks. An intern in the corner was meticulously organizing a binder, trying to appear *very* busy. Another intern was talking on the phone, holding one ear shut to cancel out the background noise.

The intern that I introduced myself to looked unenergetic and mildly confused. "Is Kevin expecting you?" Her authoritative tone annoyed me. I wanted to tell her to slap a smile on her face, greet me happily regardless of who I was, and phone Kevin.

"No. Just tell him that Sydney is here to say hello," I said with a smile.

The intern slowly got up from the main desk. When she came back, she said, "He'll be right—"

"Sydney! What are you doing here?" Kevin exclaimed, coming around the corner. *Oh, thank goodness*, I thought, *he is in a good mood*.

"Surprise! I'm here for work and wanted to stop by and say hi! Is this a good time?" I felt all eyes in the office turn on me. Being back almost made me feel like I should be doing something. I looked around at the other employees, who had stopped working.

"That's awesome of you to visit! We have never had a past intern visit. This means a lot," Kevin replied.

Wait, seriously? No intern, ever? So people spend three months or so dedicating themselves to an internship here and then disappear? I was suddenly very confused.

"Really?" I asked. "I'm surprised interns don't visit. Or at least keep in touch."

"We remember the few who do. And I had a feeling when you left that it wasn't the last time I was going to see you."

. . .

I learned during that visit how beneficial it is to keep in touch with your past employers. People understandably get busy and wrapped up in the here and now, and that's why your efforts to maintain communication and a professional relationship will be noted and appreciated. Read on to learn how to stay in touch with your mentor after your internship (without being annoying or bothersome).

THE FIRST UPDATE

Hopefully, you left your internship on good terms with your mentor and the rest of the office. Assuming that you did, congrats! This means that you probably added some new names to your network list (see "The Last Week").

About a month after your internship ends, you can begin to consider sending your mentor the first update. The tone with which you follow up with your past employer is subjective. Some interns will leave their internship and feel quite close with their mentor. Other times you'll leave without having gotten much closer than you were to your mentor on day one. Depending on your level of comfort, begin to brainstorm what you want to follow up about and how you want to come across. The following are three examples of potential follow-up notes:

+ INFORMAL TONE

Hi, Lilly,

I cannot believe it's already been a month since my last day! The last week flew by so quickly that we didn't get to really discuss the potential full-time position you mentioned for after I graduate. I just wanted to let you know that I am still very interested and would love to set up a time this week to talk about the position. Looking forward to hearing from you!

+ SEMIFORMAL TONE

Hi, Robert,

Hope all is well! I wanted to thank you again for all of your advice during my internship—I cannot believe my last day was already a month ago! I am also reaching out to discuss a potential position within the company after my graduation this spring. I enjoyed my internship so much that I would absolutely love the opportunity to join the team full-time. Let me know your thoughts—I look forward to hearing from you!

+ FORMAL TONE

Dear Hannah:

I wanted to personally thank you again for your useful advice and feedback during my internship. I learned an extensive amount of information from you that I continue to practice on a daily basis. I also wanted to connect with you about a potential full-time position within the company next summer. Let me know if an opening is available and, if so, I would be more than happy to set up a call at a time convenient for you. Looking forward to hearing from you, and thank you in advance for your consideration.

FROM INTERN TO EMPLOYEE

You may have loved your internship so much that you would consider working there after graduation. Sometimes an employer will mention a potential part-time or full-time position with the company before you leave your internship (congrats if they do!). If not, don't get discouraged. It doesn't mean the opportunity is out of the question. Refer back to the first chapter, "The Search." You might not know if the company is hiring. But remember how I said you never know until you ask? Now that your internship is over and you're staying in touch, it is an appropriate time to think about potential opportunities within that company. If you made a positive impact as an intern, chances are your mentor probably would love to have you back because you are already familiar with the company's environment and day-to-day responsibilities.

When you contact your mentor about a potential job, be concise and straightforward. State exactly what you want, and don't sugarcoat it—for example, "I am interested in a full-time position with your company beginning after my graduation this spring. Do you have any openings?"—instead of beating around the bush with something vague like "I loved my internship so much! I cannot believe I graduate in only six months. Although I am unsure of my plans after graduation, I sure hope I can work for a company that is half as great as my internship!" Remember: you want a job.

Companies want to hire people who actually *want* to work for them. Otherwise the company is setting itself up for failure: a former intern turned employee with a sour attitude and poor work ethic. That scenario does not happen too often with intern, because companies get a good feel for your work ethic and strengths during your internship. They can probably already tell if you would be a suitable fit as an employee.

THE RETURN VISIT

You might want to make an in-person appearance after your internship to say hello to the office and wish everyone well. Or you might want to return for the chance to talk about job opportunities in the future. Very rarely, your drop-in surprise visit can turn into a "We want you back" talk. Whether you schedule a drop-by or visit on a whim is very situational. For example, if you want to visit but know your mentor travels a lot for meetings, it is probably best to schedule a time to visit. Most of the time, though, a drop-by visit goes a long way with a former mentor. Your former mentor could say, however, that you are welcome back anytime for a visit. In that case, visit once every few months to keep in touch and ensure that you are not forgotten. Before the visit, it is important to think about the reason behind your drop-by. If you are stopping by just to say hello, keep the visit brief and inform your former mentor that you don't mean to interrupt but you were in the area and wanted to stop in to let it be known that you were thinking of her. If you are stopping by to discuss potential opportunities within the company, be sure to come prepared with a list of reasons why you are interested in working for the organization full-time and why you would be an exceptional candidate.

THE JOB OFFER

My return visit to my LA internship office turned into one of those rare "We want you back" talks. When I visited the city, I emailed my past employer to tell him I would love to stop by. He assured me that he would be in the office that day and that he was excited to see me.

Walking back into that office felt like going home. The employees, surprised at first, happily greeted me and said that they missed me. The feeling was mutual. So mutual, as a matter of fact, that I was called into the owner's office to discuss what I planned on doing postgraduation. Yes, the "We want you back" talk. It's an incredible and honorable talk to have, but do not accept an offer until you have all of the details— salary, bonuses (if any), other compensation, responsibilities, room for growth, travel, and so on. Take a few days to really think about what you want. Your first job offer will not be your last, so do not rush the decision. Don't be afraid to counter the offer and do not be afraid to negotiate.

FROM INTERN TO INTERN

One of my favorite parts about an internship is bonding with the other interns. Spending five days a week for eight weeks together inevitably causes you to really get to know each other. Of course you will not always get along with *every* intern. I cannot say that I was BFFs with the gal who threw away the packaging tape dispenser after the tape ran out (apparently not everyone knows to refill those things), but at least I found her entertaining. Regardless of where you intern, you will be introduced to new people from near and far. There is nothing quite like the intermixing of confused yet eager students wanting to make a positive impression and better their futures.

It takes effort to keep in touch. But I believe that it is worth the effort to stay in touch with people you connected with during your internships. Don't burn any bridges, and use your work experience with them as a networking opportunity. (Remember: everyone you need to know you already know.) For example, I met a guy through one of my fellow interns with whom I clicked right away. I kept in touch with both of them, and still do to this day. The guy ended up writing one of the best endorsements I was able to include on my résumé—from a University of Oxford postgraduate student.

To ensure that you are able to stay in touch with your fellow interns, connect with them on social media. Find them on LinkedIn and follow them on Twitter. That way you are able to keep up with their career in the industry you, too, are interested in, without emailing or texting back and forth. They might follow and communicate with a network of people in your industry with whom you would like to get in touch. Begin to view people you work with as networking resources.

. . .

View the follow-up with your employer, fellow interns, and other people you met along the way as opportunities that are just as important as the internship itself. This is your chance to take advantage of personal and professional relationships and learn from them. Too often we get wrapped up in our own worlds and forget how much it means to occasionally take time out of your day to send them a message. Not even a handwritten letter this time! Just a simple follow-up to stay fresh in their minds.

THE FOLLOW-UP TAKEAWAYS

The First Update
- Email your former mentor about a month after your internship to say thanks again for the opportunity to intern.

From Intern to Employee
- You already have experience with the company. Go ahead and ask about a part-time or full-time position.

The Return Visit
- Determine whether a scheduled drop-by or surprise visit would be most appropriate.

From Intern to Intern
- Fellow interns are a great networking resource—follow them on social media.

ABOUT THE AUTHOR

Photo © 2015 Julie Brown

Sydney N. Fulkerson graduated early and with honors from the University of Kentucky, where she earned her BS in merchandising and a minor in business. During her senior year, she wrote an internship how-to guide for students titled *The Coffee Run: And Other Internship Need-to-Knows*. Her internship expertise derived from a handful of sales and marketing internships across the country. When she's not writing and speaking to students, she's most likely finding any excuse to travel and any excuse to support her area of expertise: stimulating the economy through shopping.

NOTES

THE PREPARATION

1. US Department of Labor Wage and Hour Division, *Fact Sheet #71: Internship Programs Under the Fair Labor Standards Act*, April 2010, http://www.dol.gov/whd/regs/compliance/whdfs71.pdf.

THE FIRST WEEK

1. Sarah Stevenson, "There's Magic In Your Smile: How Smiling Affects Your Brain," *Cutting-Edge Leadership* (blog), *Psychology Today*, June 25, 2012, https://www.psychologytoday.com/blog/cutting-edge-leadership/201206/there-s-magic-in-your-smile.

2. Anthony C. Little, Benedict C. Jones, and Lisa M. DeBruine, "Facial Attractiveness: Evolutionary Based Research, *Philosophical Transactions of the Royal Society B* 366 (May 2011): 1638–1659, doi:10.1098/rstb.2010.0404.

THE STANDOUT INTERN

1. Alice Moon and Serena Chen, "The Power to Control Time: Power Influences How Much Time (You Think) You Have," *Journal of Experimental Social Psychology* 54 (September 2014): 97–101, doi:10.1016/j.jesp.2014.04.011.

2. Mashallah Valikhani and Fahimeh Karimi, "A Study of the Effect of Self-Management (Managing Themselves) on the Performance (Case Study: City Council Staff Khomeini Shahr)," *International Journal of Academic Research in Business and Social Sciences* 5, no. 1 (2015): 240–248.

THE SPONSORS

You know what sort of sucks? Asking people for money. I can't really think of one person I know who would say, "I just *love* asking people for money." Even if you are in sales and asking for money is practically hidden in your job description, the question "Would you be interested in donating to my book's publication?" was not an easy one to ask. I strongly believed in this book and its benefits, however. My passion behind this book enabled me to do all I could to reach my goal through the development of a Corporate Sponsorship Opportunity. I would like to personally thank the following people and businesses for taking part in my sponsorship opportunity to help me get this book published. I am incredibly appreciative of your support and for your belief in *The Coffee Run*.

PLATINUM SPONSOR—$500+

BECKY NEAL OCHENKOSKI
tribeca trunk

ROBERT P. SCHNEIDER
Schneider Wealth Management

GOLD SPONSORS—$250+

CHRIS FULKERSON
V.I.P. Studios—Visual Impact and Presence Image Consulting

CLARENCE CUNDIFF
Cundiff Real Estate Consultants

DAVID and CHERYL FRANCK
State Farm Insurance Agency

MIKE and INNA MARNHOUT
Bluegrass Oxygen

MYRON K. HOBBS
Epic Insurance Solutions

INKSHARES

Inkshares is a crowdfunded book publisher. We democratize publishing by having readers select the books we publish—we edit, design, print, distribute, and market any book that meets a pre-order threshold.

Interested in making a book idea come to life? Visit inkshares. com to find new book projects or to start your own.